AZTECS

& CONQUISTADORES

The Spanish Invasion
& the Collapse of the Aztec Empire

To use "Aztecs" to mean "the collective name of the Nahuatl speaking peoples of the Basin of Mexico" is somewhat analogous to using "Bostonians" to mean "the collective name of the English speaking peoples of the Thirteen Colonies."

No!

AZTECS
& CONQUISTADORES

The Spanish Invasion
& the Collapse of the ~~Aztec~~ *Triple Alliance* Empire

JOHN POHL & CHARLES M ROBINSON III

First published in Great Britain in 2005 by Osprey Publishing, Midland House, West Way, Botley, Oxford, OX2 0PH, United Kingdom.
443 Park Avenue South, New York, NY 10016, USA.
Email: info@ospreypublishing.com

Previously published as Warrior 32: *Aztec Warrior AD 1325–1521*, Warrior 40: *The Conquistador 1492–1550*, and Essential Histories 60: *The Spanish Invasion of Mexico 1519–1521*.

A CIP catalog record for this book is available from the British Library

ISBN 1 84176 934 7

Page Layout by Ken Vail Graphic Design, Cambridge, UK
Index by David Worthington
Maps by The Map Studio
Originated by PPS Grasmere Ltd, Leeds, UK
Printed in China through Worldprint Ltd

05 06 07 08 09   10 9 8 7 6 5 4 3 2 1

For a catalog of all books published by Osprey please contact:

NORTH AMERICA
Osprey Direct, 2427 Bond Street, University Park, IL 60466, USA
E-mail: info@ospreydirectusa.com

ALL OTHER REGIONS
Osprey Direct UK, P.O. Box 140, Wellingborough, Northants, NN8 2FA, UK
E-mail: info@ospreydirect.co.uk

www.ospreypublishing.com

Front cover: Massacre of the Mexicans by Diego Durán. (Bridgeman Art Library)
Back cover: John Pohl
Endpapers and title page: American Museum of Natural History
Contents page: Ann Ronan Picture Library/Heritage-Images.

CONTENTS

INTRODUCTION

7

PART ONE
BACKGROUND TO THE WAR

17

PART TWO
WARRING SIDES

33

PART THREE
THE SPANISH INVASION OF MEXICO

93

CONCLUSION
NEW SPAIN AND NEW LEGACIES

157

BIBLIOGRAPHY AND FURTHER READING

171

GLOSSARY

175

INDEX

178

INTRODUCTION

The Spanish Conquest of Mexico completely changed the history of the world. The establishment of a European power on the mainland of the western hemisphere opened the door for a complete European hegemony, ultimately leading to the establishment of independent states. Whether this was for better or worse is debatable, however now, some 500 years later, a western hemisphere nation is the dominant power in the world. And while the United States may be the cultural heir to Great Britain, to a large extent it has inherited civilizing influences from Spain, too: fully one-third of the nation was once a part of "New Spain," as the Spaniards came to call Mexico. San Antonio, Texas, Santa Fe, New Mexico, and Monterey, California, were all seats of Spanish government until 1821, and of Mexican government until even later, and Spanish and English are spoken side by side throughout the American southwest. This is the legacy of Columbus, Hernán Cortés and the other Conquistadores.

The marriage of King Ferdinand and Queen Isabella in 1469 joined the Iberian kingdoms of Aragón and Castile and began a course of Spanish expansion that would lead to the defeat of the Islamic Emirate of Granada, the discovery of the Americas, and the invasion of Italy. In 1492, Christopher Columbus had returned from Española (Haiti-Santo Domingo) with reports of new lands populated by an indigenous people who possessed no metal tools or weapons but a great deal of gold. In 1493, he established a colony of 1,500 men, but he was unable to deal with divisive factions among both the Spanish colonists and the Arawak Indian people. Open revolts ensued that led to the ruthless military subjugation of the island of Española, only concluding with Columbus's own arrest. Succeeding administrators were hardly more competent and just as murderous. Under Friar Nicolás de Ovando, Anacoana, the wife of a paramount Arawak chief, was hanged and other rebellious leaders were burned alive. Ovando then instituted the *encomienda* system by which large numbers of the Indian population were condemned to work in permanent

Hernán Cortés (1485–1547). Ruthless, single-minded and ambitious, Cortés's determination and bravery established the Spanish hegemony in the New World, and destroyed the Aztec civilization. His intelligence and ability to work with Indian allies meant that his expedition succeeded where others had failed. (Ann Ronan Picture Library/Heritage-Images)

servitude to Spanish landowners. In 1509, Columbus's son, Diego, was appointed governor. Unable to control the ambitions of wealthy landowners like Ponce de León, Esquivel, Narváez and Velásquez, the first Conquistadores overran Puerto Rico, Jamaica, and Cuba in three short years, killing anyone and anything that got in the way of their search for gold.

For years Muslim princes had paid tribute in the precious yellow metal and had fashioned magnificent objects of art and ornamentation from it. But by the 15th century European monarchs wanted to emulate the Florentines and produce gold coinage. Gold soon began to haunt the imagination of Spaniards as the one commodity that could transcend the oppressive limitations of social rank. Columbus bluntly stated that a man with enough gold could even take souls to paradise. Yet by 1519, the Spanish Main was a pitiful shell of its former prosperity. Most of the gold placers had been worked out, and the Arawak Indian people, the real wealth of the land, had been mercilessly exploited on plantations and ranches. Disease was rampant, reducing the Arawak population of Española alone from one million in 1492 to less than 16,000 in 1518. It was clear that the Spanish would have to venture further afield if they were to find the gold they sought.

In the spring of 1519, Hernán Cortés, a failed law student turned planter and speculator, led the third expedition in as many years to explore Mexico. He and 600 adventurers embarked on the conquest of a ruthless and predatory empire with an army numbering in the tens of thousands. The Spanish conquest of Mexico was the greatest military expedition in history, and in achieving it, Cortés proved himself one of the foremost generals of all time. However, the Conquest was not simply a war between soldiers, but a confrontation between civilizations and between belief systems. The Aztecs' own fatalism and obsession with ritual played a major part in their downfall. They knew that their gods were demanding and capricious, who could give or withhold their beneficence on a whim. They believed that the world had been destroyed four times before. It would be destroyed again. The Aztecs themselves were foreigners who had displaced the native peoples of the valley, and they too would be displaced. There had been prophecies of doom, and there had been omens. Now it seemed as though all the elements of their destruction were falling into place. Yet they would hold out and fight until the end, because they were warriors who accepted the decisions of their gods without question.

On the Spanish side, Cortés's men fought with grim desperation, when the object was no longer riches, nor even their lives, but the fate of their souls. They knew full well that if captured, they would be dragged to the tops of the temples and offered up as sacrifices to idols that they literally believed were manifestations of Satan and his demons. They had seen these monstrous idols covered in blood, described as demons by Old Testament prophets, in the Revelation of St. John, and by a thousand years of Christianity. Yet they also knew, through the teachings of Christ, that in the end they must triumph. In their own lifetimes they had witnessed the end of eight centuries of Islam in Spain. And in overthrowing the idols and conquering the idolaters they believed they were carrying Christ's mandate to take His word to all the world. If they died, sword in hand, fighting against these demon gods, their salvation was assured.

CHRONOLOGY

1469   Ferdinand of Aragón and Isabella of Castile marry, and the unification of Spain follows.

1484   Birth of Hernán Cortés.

1491–92   Ferdinand and Isabella defeat the Moors under Muhammad XI Boabdil at Granada.

Columbus, together with Vicente Yáñez Pinzón and his brother Martín Alonso, land at Española. The Spaniards form an alliance with the Arawak chief Guacanagari and found the town of La Natividad on the island's northwestern coast.

1493   Maximilian Habsburg becomes Holy Roman Emperor as Maximilian I.

1493–96   Columbus makes a second voyage to Española. He finds La Natividad has been destroyed, the colonists having been put to death by a hostile faction of Arawaks. The Spaniards found a second community at La Isabela 60 miles to the east. The colony is beset by hurricanes, epidemics, and fire. Open warfare again breaks out with the Arawaks over demands for labor and tribute in gold. Columbus's brother

Bartholomew founds Santo Domingo on the southern coast.
Huayna Capac becomes emperor of the Inca Empire.

1495   Ferdinand and Isabella dispatch an army to defend Aragón's claims to Sicily and southern Italy against Charles VIII of France. For the next ten years, the Spaniards, under such remarkable commanders as Gonzalo Fernández de Córdoba, participate in wars between the French, the Holy Roman Empire, the Pope, and the Italian city states.

1497   Francisco Roldán leads an insurrection against Columbus. His faction of La Isabela colonists move west to ally themselves with an Arawak faction under paramount chief Behechio and his sister Anacoana.

1498–1500   Columbus makes a third voyage of exploration to South America. He is returned to Spain in chains after being accused of administrative incompetence and corruption.

1499–1500   Vicente Yáñez Pinzón carries out slave raids along the north coast of Columbia, confirming the existence of the South American continent.

1502–04   Columbus embarks on a fourth and final voyage of exploration following the coast of Honduras, Nicaragua, Costa Rica and Panama. He encounters Indian canoe traffic in rich luxury goods providing first evidence of the tremendous wealth of Mesoamerican civilizations. Motecuhzoma II is elected Aztec emperor at age 34.

1503   Gonzalo de Córdoba defeats the Marquis di Saluzzo at the battle of Garigliano forcing the French to withdraw from Italy. Battle-hardened veterans return to Spain where they learn of the new-found wealth of the "Indies." Some, including the future Conquistador of Peru, Francisco de Pizarro, are encouraged to redirect their military talents to the invasion of the western hemisphere.

Operating under orders from Nicolás de Ovando, the governor of Santo Domingo in Española, Diego de Velásquez executes Anacoana and 80 subordinate chiefs, completing the subjugation of western Española.

1504   Queen Isabella dies.

Juan de Esquivel and Juan Ponce de León conquer eastern Española and the island is made a Spanish colony. Plantations and ranches replace gold mining as the primary economic ventures. Increased demand for slave labor to work the land fosters further expansion throughout the Caribbean.

1504–06   Juan de la Cosa, Alonso de Hojeda, Diego de Nicuesa and others attempt to establish settlements on the mainland of Central and South America with variable success. Abandoned by Hojeda, Francisco de Pizarro establishes a settlement at Urabá, Colombia. Hostilities with local chiefs subsequently force the Spaniards to relocate to Darién.

1506   Columbus dies. Hernán Cortés embarks from Spain for Española.

1508   Vicente Yáñez Pinzón and Juan Díaz de Solis explore the coast of Honduras and the Yucatán Peninsula confirming the existence of Mesoamerica to the east.

1509   Ponce de León subdues Puerto Rico. Juan de Esquivel and Pánfilo de Narváez conquer Jamaica.

1511	Traveling from Darien to Española, Gonzalo Guerrero and Geronimo de Aguilar are shipwrecked on the Yucatán Peninsula. Guerrero eventually becomes a Maya warlord and leads troops against the Spaniards in many subsequent battles. Aguilar becomes Cortés's translator after he is rescued in 1519.
1512–14	Diego Velásquez de Cuellar and Pánfilo de Narváez conquer Cuba. Cortés participates, gaining invaluable knowledge of how to conduct campaigns against Indian armies. Velásquez is appointed governor. Cortés serves as his secretary and later gains wealth through cattle and gold enterprises.
1513	On a mission to locate new sources of gold, pearls, and slaves, Vasco Nuñez de Balboa crosses the Isthmus of Panama thereby opening up the Pacific coast to Spanish expansionism. Pizarro participates in the expedition. Ponce de León explores Florida.
1515	Francis I becomes king of France and initiates new campaigns in Italy. Spain engages in ten years of nearly continuous warfare on the Italian peninsula.
1516	Ferdinand dies. His daughter's son, Charles, succeeds him as the first king of a united Spain. Three years later, Charles is elected Holy Roman Emperor as Charles V upon the death of his paternal grandfather, Maximilian I.
1517	Acting on reports of rich lands to the east, Governor Velásquez sends Córdoba to explore the Yucatán Peninsula. He returns only after suffering numerous casualties at the hands of the Chontal, and dies of wounds shortly after.
1518	Encouraged by reports of vast populations living in cities, Velásquez sends a second expedition under Juan de Grijalva. Lacking the necessary supplies to carry out any protracted campaign along the coast of Yucatán or Tabasco, Grijalva reaches Veracruz and decides to return to Cuba. **October** Velásquez commissions Hernán Cortés to lead a third expedition. **November** Cortés sails from Santiago de Cuba, in defiance of the governor. Finishes fitting out at Trinidad and San Cristóbal de la Habana.
1519	**February 10** Cortés sails for Mexico. He traverses the Gulf coast and eventually lands at Veracruz where he allies himself with the Totonacs. **April** Cortés founds the settlement of Villa Rica. **June** Cortés departs from Cempoala for the Mexican interior. **July** Members of the expedition petition the Crown for recognition as a separate colony. **August–September** War in Tlaxcala; alliance formed with Tlaxcalteca. **October–November** Allied with the Tlaxcalteca, Cortés enters Tenochtitlán and seizes Motecuhzoma as a hostage. The city of Panama is founded. Magellan embarks on a three-year voyage around the world. Nuñez de Balboa is beheaded for treason in Panama. Uprising against Spaniards on the coast. **December** The instigator of the uprising, Cualpopoca, is burned at the stake in Tenochtitlán by the Spaniards.

This painting depicts the retreat of Hernán Cortés from Tenochtitlán in 1520. From the British Embassy Collection, Mexico City. (Ann Ronan Picture Library/Heritage-Images)

1520

April Charles V receives the petition for recognition of the Cortés expedition as a separate colonial venture. An expeditionary force from Cuba under Pánfilo Narváez lands with orders to arrest Cortés and break up his expedition; Cortés leaves Mexico to confront Narváez, leaving Pedro de Alvarado in command.

May Alvarado fires on the crowds during the Toxcatl celebration in the Temple Square. Cortés defeats Narváez near Cempoala.

June 24 Cortés returns to Mexico. Spaniards under siege.

June Motecuhzoma deposed. Cuitláhuac elected emperor. Motecuhzoma dies, probably of injuries received from stoning by angry crowds.

June 30 *La Noche Triste*. Cortés leads his expedition out of Mexico. Caught on the causeway, many are slaughtered by the Mexicans.

Summer–Autumn Smallpox epidemic breaks out. Cuitláhuac dies. Cuauhtémoc elected emperor.

June 30–July 10 Retreat from Mexico to Tlaxcala.

July 7 Battle of Otumba. Spanish cavalry saves expedition from complete annihilation.

August–September Cortés prepares for return to Mexico. Segura de la Frontera founded at Tepeac as a base.

December 26 Cortés begins advance toward Mexico from Segura.

1521

April Cortés besieges Tenochtitlán with an army of over 900 Spaniards and ultimately more than 50,000 Indian allies.

A *tzompantli* represented in stone at the Templo Mayor (Great Temple) in Mexico. (Topfoto)

May Gonzalo de Sandoval moves toward Iztapalapa, beginning the siege of Mexico.

May–August Siege continues.

August Cuauhtémoc surrenders; Aztec empire ends.

Ponce de León dies of wounds after his second expedition to Florida.

1522 **October** Charles V names Cortés governor and captain general of New Spain (Mexico).

1522–23 Cortés leads an expedition into West Mexico. Pedro de Alvarado, Cortés's former second-in-command, attacks the city-states of Mixtec and Zapotec in Oaxaca, then embarks on a campaign against the highland Maya of Guatemala. He ceases hostilities upon confronting a formidable Pipil army in El Salvador.

1524–26 Velásquez dies. Cortés embarks on a punitive expedition after Cristóbal de Olid in Honduras and traverses Guatemala's Petén jungle. The last Aztec emperor, Cuauhtémoc, is taken along as hostage, but is executed. Francisco Pizarro leads an expedition south into Colombia.

Spanish and Imperial troops defeat the French at the battle of Pavia, Italy.

1526–27   Pizarro makes a second expedition, sailing as far south as Ecuador where he trades for gold, llamas, and other luxury goods, tangible proof of the existence of a vast Inca empire in Peru. Inca Emperor Huayna Capac dies of smallpox. His sons, Atahualpa and Huascar, dispute the inheritance to the Incan empire. Francisco de Montejo initiates his campaign against the Maya of the Yucatán Peninsula.

1528   Cortés returns to Spain where both he and Pizarro meet with Emperor Charles. Cortés is appointed Marquis of the Valley of Oaxaca. Pizarro is commissioned to invade the Incan empire.
Succeeding Velásquez as governor of Cuba, Narváez leads a doomed expedition to Florida. An officer named Cabeza de Vaca is among a handful of survivors who reach Mexico after eight years of Indian captivity and wandering. His report inspires both the de Soto and Coronado expeditions.

1529–30   Nuño de Guzmán subjugates West Mexico.
The Treaty of Cambrai concludes hostilities between France, Spain, Italy, and the Holy Roman Empire in Europe.

1531–35   Pizarro leads an army of 160 men into Peru. Hernando de Soto serves as cavalry commander. Upon hearing that Atahualpa is marching south to crown himself emperor in Cuzco, Pizarro intercepts the monarch and executes him. The Spaniards then embark on an 800-mile campaign, fighting their way into the Inca capital where they govern for two years through Huayna Capac's son, Manco. Lima is later founded as the new Spanish capital of Peru. Cortés leads an expedition to the Gulf of California. Francisco de Montejo campaigns in Tabasco and Campeche.

1535   Conquistadores displaced by bureaucrats. Antonio de Mendoza becomes first viceroy of New Spain, inaugurating an administrative system that lasts until 1821.

1539–42   Hernando de Soto leaves Cuba, invades Florida, then moves north and east making war on largely Muskogean Indian nations from Georgia to Louisiana until he dies from fever. Luis de Moscoso assumes command of the expedition and flees to Veracruz. Juan Rodriguez Cabrillo explores the Pacific coast of California and Oregon.

1540–42   Francisco Vásquez de Coronado invades the southwestern United States. He wages campaigns against the Zuni and Rio Grande Pueblo Indian peoples among others until he realizes there is little fortune to be gained and returns to Mexico.

1541   Pedro de Alvarado dies of wounds near Guadalajara, Mexico. Pizarro is assassinated at Lima, Peru.

1547   Cortés dies at Castilleja de la Cuesta outside Seville, Spain.

PART ONE

BACKGROUND TO THE WAR

SPAIN

At the beginning of the 16th century Spain had only recently emerged from almost eight centuries of civil wars, collectively called the *Reconquista*, or the Moorish Wars, when the northern kingdoms of the Iberian peninsula, Castile and Aragón, fought to recover the land conquered by the Moors in the 8th century. In 1492 Granada, the last bastion of Islamic rule, was recovered and in the same year Spain's Jewish population faced the choice between expulsion or conversion to Christianity. Although the *Reconquista* was regarded by Christian Spaniards as the expulsion of foreigners, the Moors had become such an integral part of Spanish society that they could no longer be called foreign. The same could be said of the nation's extensive Jewish population, which had made substantial contributions to philosophy, science, and economics.

During the final years of the Reconquest, the idea of Spain as a unified nation was a concept rather than a fact. The Iberian peninsula was essentially divided between three dominant kingdoms: Portugal to the west, Castile down the center, and Aragón to the east. Of the three, Portugal was the wealthiest and most powerful, but the least interested in Iberian affairs, being preoccupied with the developing African empire that was the source of its wealth and power. The others, Castile and Aragón, had managed to swallow most of the lesser kingdoms, leaving only two – Christian Navarre to the north, and Muslim Granada to the south – maintaining a precarious independence. A dynastic marriage between Queen Isabella of Castile and Crown Prince Ferdinand of Aragón in 1469 spelled the end of these two minor kingdoms and the conception, if not the birth, of a united Spain.

The first to fall was Granada, which surrendered in January 1492. This event, and the successful first voyage of Christopher Columbus of 1492–93, created a new sense of optimism, nationalism, and religious xenophobia. The Spaniards now saw themselves on

A woodcut illustrating Protestants, Moors, and Jews being burned alive. During the late 15th century, Ferdinand and Isabella attempted to forge a Spanish national identity by persecuting all non-Catholics. This ruthless policy of self-righteousness and intolerance was enacted with the same zeal by their representatives in the western hemisphere and had an equally devastating effect on the indigenous peoples. (Illustration by John Pohl)

a great national adventure tinged with religious evangelism. Patriotism and religious fervor were spurred ever onward by the promise of wealth. The first generation of voyagers – Columbus and his companions – were followed by an even more eager second generation. Between 1506 and 1518 some 200 ships made the passage from Spain to the Indies in search of new lands.

There were other, more tangible, motives. The leaders of expeditions of discovery and conquest often were members of the minor nobility, men with more pedigree than money or influence, who hoped to establish themselves both financially and politically by venturing to the Indies. The rank and file emigrated because farming in Castile had been replaced by the less labor-intensive stock raising. Many ordinary Castilians of the early 1500s faced poverty and hunger. Finally, there was the desire to be free not only of the established hierarchy of Church and nobility but of the growing new state bureaucracy as well.

For all the optimism and adventure, however, the discovery of what rapidly came to be called the New World was a traumatic event, not only for the Indians about to encounter European domination, but for the Europeans as well. Although the Renaissance brought an advance of culture and classical learning, the Europeans were totally unprepared for the discovery of new continents and their people. When their history, science, and philosophy could not explain the New World or its people, they turned to religion for answers to the unanswerable. It took centuries to truly understand what had happened, if, indeed, it is even yet understood. Faced with native peoples unlike any humans they had ever encountered, the Europeans were unsure whether they

A man of his time, Christopher Columbus has been seen by some modern schoalars as ignorant, blundering, vain and avaricious. Columbus set the disastrous and irreversible course of Spanish military policy in the Caribbean. (Ancient Art and Architecture)

were of God or of the Devil. Did they have souls? Were they even human or merely a higher species of animal? The fact that the Indians themselves had, over thousands of years, developed a culture isolated from the rest of humanity and therefore alien to any conventional understanding, only aggravated the issues.

By 1517 Spaniards had established themselves not only in their initial foothold in Española, but in Darien (Panama), Jamaica, Puerto Rico, and Cuba as well. Slaving expeditions had ventured into the islands of the Gulf of Honduras and along the coasts of Nicaragua and Florida. The western Gulf of Mexico and northwestern Caribbean, however, were a void. To fill that void, the governor of Cuba, Don Diego Velásquez, commissioned two expeditions to investigate the region. The first, led by Francisco Hernández de Córdoba attempted to land in Tabasco in 1517 but was attacked by the Maya. His men were nearly annihilated and he himself later died of his wounds. However, reports of societies of people living in great cities convinced Velásquez to finance another expedition under his nephew, Juan de Grijalva, the following year. Like Córdoba, Grijalva also encountered strong resistance to landings within Maya territory, but found willing trading partners further north among both the Aztec and Totonac

The Invasion of Cuba

By the early 16th century, much of the indigenous population of Española was dying from war, disease, and labor on the *encomiendas*, so the Conquistadores began to explore other islands in search of slaves as well as gold. After conquering the southeastern part of Española, Ponce de León learned that there was gold as well as a large population of Arawaks on the island of Puerto Rico and applied for permission to investigate. By 1509, he had subjugated the Indians, enslaved many of them, and looted enough gold to make him one of the richest men in the Caribbean. His success encouraged others to engage in similar enterprises. Two years later, Diego Velásquez de Cuéllar overran Cuba, carrying out numerous unprovoked massacres of the Indian population just as he had

on Española. It was here that Cortés was to gain his most valuable military experience. Dogs played a critical part in these campaigns as they were adept at breaking up ambushes in dense forests, giving the Spaniards time to reposition themselves for defense. Usually wolf hounds, dogs had first been employed as early as 1493 and proved so effective that some regarded them as being equal to ten men against Arawak warriors armed only with spears. Among the most famous was Becerrillo or "Little Calf" who reputedly killed so many that he earned for Ponce de León an additional crossbowman's pay and one and a half shares of booty. Other Conquistadores, including Cortés, later executed their prisoners by turning the "dogs of war" on them. (Adam Hook © Osprey Publishing Ltd)

peoples of Veracruz. It soon became clear that there were divisive factions at work in mainland Indian politics, an observation that Cortés later noted and exploited.

Córdoba and Grijalva had formally taken possession of the coasts of Yucatán and Campeche on behalf of the Crown, and Velásquez, who had applied to Spain for proconsulship of the newly discovered regions, decided a third expedition was in order, to be commanded by Hernán Cortés. Although Velásquez distrusted Cortés, and the latter's military experience was limited to the relatively simple conquest of Cuba, he was nevertheless a powerfully wealthy force in Cuban politics and a shrewd judge of men. He had money and credit to risk, while the governor was loathe to risk his own. It is doubtful whether anyone envisioned that his appointment would change the history of the world – except, perhaps, Cortés himself.

This remarkable man was born in Medellín in 1485, the son of Don Martín Cortés de Monroy, and his wife, Doña Catalina Pizarro de Altamirano, both members of minor nobility. As a youth, he was sickly, and nearly died several times. In the religiously charged atmosphere of the era, his survival was attributed to St. Peter, whom he invoked on any great undertaking in later life. At 14 he was sent to the university at Salamanca, where he studied law, and, although capable, was bored and indifferent. After two years he used lack of funds and chronic illness as an excuse to drop out and return home. After that he wandered aimlessly about Spain for a year, no doubt hearing stories of the Indies from sailors and adventurers in the country's southern ports. In 1504 he set sail for Santo Domingo, where he obtained a grant of land and Indians. Through a family friendship with the governor, Don Nicolás de Ovando, Cortés also was appointed notary of the town council of Azúa, a position with actual legal power when compared to its English or American counterparts.

By 1511 Cortés was a successful planter in Santo Domingo. Nevertheless, he accompanied Velásquez in the conquest of Cuba, serving as clerk to the treasurer. He received a grant of Indians which he shared with Juan Juárez, whose sister, Catalina, he married. Cortés's position soon brought him into conflict with Velásquez. Both were strong willed and each was determined to be the dominant force in Cuban affairs. Cortés headed a faction that quietly worked to undermine Velásquez, and the shrewd governor was fully aware of it. Neither, however, was strong enough to subvert the other, and an uneasy alliance ensued, occasionally punctuated by open feuding. This was one of the considerations that prompted Velásquez to place Cortés in charge of the expedition to Mexico: he had a competent man in charge, while at the same time he rid himself of a nuisance. He little realized that he was letting the jinni out of the bottle.

Aztecatl, "a person associated with the town of Aztlan" (i.e., born in, raised in, dweller of, based in)

THE AZTECS

The name "Aztec" is debated *[should be]* by scholars today. The word *[use of the]* is not really indigenous, *NO* though it does have a cultural basis. It was first proposed by a European, the explorer- — *Clavijero* naturalist Alexander von Humboldt, and later popularized by William H. Prescott in his remarkable 1843 publication, *The History of the Conquest of Mexico*. Aztec is simply an eponym derived from Aztlan, meaning "Place of the ~~White Heron~~," a legendary homeland of seven desert tribes called Chichimecs who miraculously emerged from caves located at the heart of a sacred mountain far to the north of the Valley of Mexico. They enjoyed a peaceful existence hunting and fishing until they were divinely inspired to fulfill a destiny of conquest by their gods. They journeyed until one day they witnessed a tree being ripped asunder by a bolt of lightning. The seventh and last tribe, more properly called the Mexica, took the event as a sign that they were to divide and follow their own destiny. They continued to wander for many more years, sometimes hunting and sometimes settling down to farm, but never remaining in any one place for very long. After the collapse of Tula, the capital of a Toltec state that dominated Central Mexico from the 9th to the 13th centuries, they decided to move south to Lake Texcoco.

Impoverished and without allies, the Mexica were soon subjected to attacks by local Toltec warlords who forced them to retreat to an island where they witnessed a miraculous vision of prophecy; an eagle standing on a cactus growing from solid rock. It was the sign for Tenochtitlán, their final destination. Having little to offer other than their reputation as fearsome warriors, the Mexica had no other choice than to hire themselves out as mercenaries to rival Toltec factions. Eventually they were able to affect the balance of power in the region to such a degree that they were granted royal marriages. The Mexica, now the most powerful of the seven original Aztec tribes, incorporated their former rivals and together they conquered an empire. Eventually, they gave their name to the nation of Mexico, while their city of Tenochtitlán became what we know as Mexico City today. Historians still apply the term Aztec to the archaeological culture that dominated the Basin of Mexico, but recognize that the people themselves were highly diversified ethnically.

Tenochtitlán was divided into four districts. Each district was composed of neighborhood wards of land-owning families called *calpulli*, an Aztec term meaning simply "house groups." Most of the *calpulli* were inhabited by farmers who cultivated bountiful crops of corn, beans, and squash with an ingenious system of raised fields called *chinampas*, while others were occupied by skilled crafts people. Six major canals ran through the metropolis with many smaller canals that crisscrossed the entire city allowing one to travel virtually anywhere by boat, the principal means of economic transportation to the island. Scholars estimate that between 200,000 and 250,000 people lived in Tenochtitlán in 1500, more than four times the population of London at that time.

The Spaniards who first entered Tenochtitlán with Cortés marveled at the broad boulevards and canals, the temples dedicated to countless gods, as well as the magnificent residences of the lords and priests who resided with the emperor and attended his court. The more worldly veterans of Italian wars compared the city to Venice but were no less astonished to find such a metropolis on the other side of the world. There was a central market where thousands of people sold everything from gold, silver, gems, shell and feathers to unhewn stone, adobe bricks, and timber. Each street was devoted to a special commodity from clay pottery to dyed textiles, and a special court of

The siege of Coixtlahuaca, AD 1458

Between 1300 and 1450, Coixtlahuaca had become one of the richest kingdoms in Mesoamerica by controlling the principal trade routes that linked the Central Mexican Highlands with Veracruz, Oaxaca, and Chiapas. Every year merchants from all over Mesoamerica attended this kingdom's great market to trade in gold, turquoise, tropical bird feathers, cacao, scarlet cochineal dye, and even a special fabric made from woven rabbit hair. Lord Atonal wielded tremendous political power by negotiating alliances between the Mixtecs, the Chocho-Popoloca, the Eastern Nahua, and half-a-dozen other ethnic groups that occupied the region. Searching for an excuse to dismantle this ancient confederacy, the Aztecs accused Atonal of assassinating a hundred and sixty of their merchants. Motecuhzoma I and Nezahualcoyotl then organized an army of 300,000 men of whom no fewer than 100,000 served as porters for what would become the Triple Alliance's first long-distance campaign. Lord Atonal battles Aztec squadrons employing broad, light-weight scaling-frames of bound cane or timber. The king himself wears the turquoise crown of a Toltec *tecuhtli* as well as a long *xicolli* favored by Mixtec noblemen. The prince with whom he is defending the ramparts is a Chocho ally who wears a crown of woven fiber and a special short *ichcahuipilli* of quilted cotton. The former is based on an image from the *Lienzo Seler II* while the latter appears in the Selden Roll. Both manuscripts are pictorial histories attributed to Coixtlahuaca artists. Atonal fought valiantly but the Aztec host soundly defeated him before his allies could come to his aid. The doomed king was garroted and many of his men were executed in rituals before the Great Temple at Tenochtitlán. (Adam Hook © Osprey Publishing Ltd)

judges enforced strict rules of transaction. All manner of foods were bartered; dogs, rabbits, deer, turkeys, quail, and every sort of vegetable and fruit.

There were also three major causeways that ran from the mainland into the city. These were spanned with drawbridges that when taken up, sealed the city off entirely for defense. Freshwater was transported by a system of aqueducts of which the main construction ran from a spring on a mountain called Chapultepec on a promontory to the west. Even though the four districts had temples dedicated to the principal Aztec gods, all were overshadowed by the Great Temple, a man-made mountain constructed within the central precinct and topped by dual shrines dedicated to the Toltec storm god Tlaloc and the Chichimec war god Huitzilopochtli. The surrounding precinct itself was a city within a city of over 1200 square meters of temples, public buildings, palaces, and plazas enclosed by a defensive bastion called the *coatepantli* or serpent wall, so named after the scores of carved stone snake heads that ornamented its exterior.

Tenochtitlán was officially founded in 1325 but it would be over a century before the city rose to its height as an imperial capital. Between 1372 and 1428 the Mexica overlords called *huey tlatoque* or "great speakers," Acamapichtli, Huitzilihuitl, and Chimalpopoca served as the vassals of a despotic Tepanec lord named Tezozomoc of Azcapotzalco. Sharing in the spoils of victory they succeeded in expanding their own domain south and east along the lake. However, when Tezozomoc died in 1427, his son Maxtla seized power and had Chimalpopoca assassinated. The Mexica quickly appointed Chimalpopoca's uncle, a war captain named Itzcoatl, as *tlatoani*. Itzcoatl allied himself with the deposed heir to the throne of Texcoco, the Acolhua kingdom lying on the eastern shore of the lake, Lord Nezahualcoyotl. Together the two kings attacked Azcapotzalco. The seige lasted for over a hundred days and only concluded when Maxtla relinquished his throne and retreated into exile. Itzcoatl and Nezahualcoyotl then rewarded the Tepanec lords of Tlacopán who had aided them in overthrowing the tyrant. The three cities of Tenochtitlán, Texcoco, and Tlacopán formulated the new Aztec Empire of the Triple Alliance.

Itzcoatl died in 1440 and was succeeded by his nephew Motecuhzoma Ilhuicamina. Motecuhzoma I, as he was later known, charted the course for Aztec expansionism for the remainder of the 15th century. To the west of the Basin of Mexico lay the formidable Tarascans who dominated a rich trade in luxury goods that moved along the Pacific coast by sea-going sailing rafts from South America to the Baja Peninsula. To the south and east were wealthy confederacies dominated by the Zapotecs, Mixtecs, and Eastern Nahuas, the latter being kinsmen of the Aztecs but no less bitter rivals for domination of the Southern Mexican highlands. The high priest Tlacaelel counseled Motecuhzoma that the imperial armies would fare better by first establishing bases of operation on the peripheries of these more powerful states. Motecuhzoma therefore initiated campaigns into Morelos and Guerrero from which his imperial armies could later launch sustained attacks for months or even years at a time.

Shortly after acceding to the throne, Motecuhzoma had demanded that all the city-states of the Basin of Mexico prove their loyalty to Tenochtitlán by contributing materials

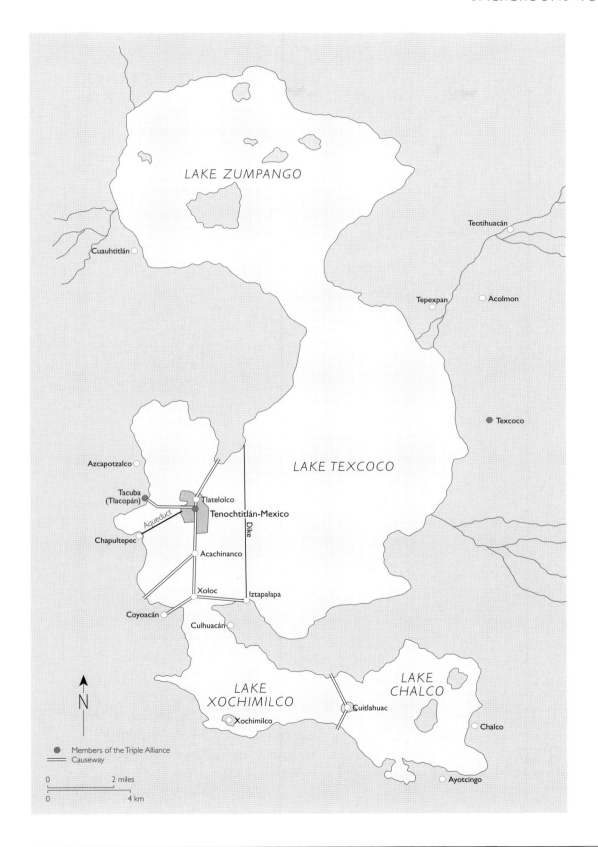

LAKE ZUMPANGO

Teotihuacán

Cuauhtitlán

Tepexpan ○ Acolmon

● Texcoco

Azcapotzalco ○

LAKE TEXCOCO

Tacuba
(Tlacopán) ●

Tlatelolco

Tenochtitlán-Mexico

Aqueduct

Dike

Chapultepec ●

Acachinanco

Xoloc

Iztapalapa

Coyoacán ○

Culhuacán ○

LAKE
XOCHIMILCO

LAKE
CHALCO

N

Cuitlahuac

Xochimilco

Chalco ○

● Members of the Triple Alliance
━━ Causeway

Ayotcingo ○

0   2 miles
0   4 km

and labor for the construction of the Great Temple dedicated to the ancient Toltec storm god Tlaloc and the Chichimec hero Huitzilopochtli. Being allied with both the Mixtecs and the Eastern Nahua, the city-state of Chalco refused and this powerful kingdom was subjugated in 1453. Choosing to avoid a confrontation with the Eastern Nahuas of Tlaxcala directly, the Aztecs then moved against the Huaxtecs and Totonacs of the Atlantic Gulf Coast. Using a variety of ingenious strategies, imperial armies soon overran much of northern Veracruz thereby assuring the empire rich tribute in exotic shell, cotton, cacao, gold, and the priceless feathers of tropical birds. Alarmed by these bold encircling maneuvers, the Eastern Nahua prepared themselves for a direct attack against Tlaxcala, Huexotzinco, or even the great pilgrimage center of the Toltec man-god Quetzalcoatl at Cholula, but the Aztecs bided their time.

In AD 1458, an Aztec imperial army initiated another "end run," marching 500 miles (800km) south from the Basin of Mexico to lay siege to the Mixtec kingdom of Coixtlahuaca, Oaxaca. According to various accounts, the expedition was organized by Motecuhzoma Ilhuicamina to avenge the murder of 160 merchants by Coixtlahuaca's Lord Atonal. However, at 300,000, the invasion force was clearly intended as more than simply a punitive expedition. Atonal immediately summoned the help of numerous Mixtec kingdoms including Teposcolula, Tilantongo, and Tlaxiaco as well as the Eastern Nahua city-states of Cholula, Huexotzinco, and Tlaxcala, with whom Coixtlahuaca was confederated; but the plea was sent too late. Coixtlahuaca was defeated before relief could arrive. Atonal was garroted and many of his men were captured and later sacrificed before the Great Temple of Tenochtitlán. Scores of city-states and kingdoms throughout Puebla and Oaxaca were stunned by the defeat. It was the beginning of the end of an era of unprecedented independence and prosperity throughout Mesoamerica.

Motecuhzoma was succeeded by his son Axayacatl in 1468. As a prince, the successor had proven himself a capable military commander by leading an expedition against the Zapotecs of Tehuantepec; now he sought to capitalize on the conquests of his illustrious father by entirely surrounding the kingdom of Tlaxcala and expanding imperial control over the Huaxtecs and Mixtecs. According to legend Axayacatl and his uncle Tlacaelel commissioned a new monument for Tenochtitlán's central religious precinct, a great round stone carved with the image of the sun dedicated to war and the conquests of the empire. As tradition dictated they received aid in the form of materials and labor from Nezahualcoyotl of Texcoco, Totoquihuaztli of Tacuba, and the other Aztec city states:

> Once this stone had been put in place, all the principal men who were present discussed the way the festivities would be held for the inauguration of the Sun Stone and where captives could be brought for sacrifice during these ceremonies. Axayacatl and Tlacaelel requested that their guests stay another day in Tenochtitlán so that they could propose to those allies that a war be waged against Michoacán. (Durán 1994: 277)

tequihua

tequihua

tequihua

mezquita

tianguez

lugar de mercados

casa

casa

casa

tequihua

tequihua

tequihua

esta partida
es el pu del
cacig de atlas
contenido g se
emplazada de
guerra por ser
rrebelde al se
ñorio de mex/
las figuras delos
tequihua / significa
ser enbiados por
el s. de mx a dre
pueblo yg los pagen de modo ocultamete
yga g segun mundo ytlabaro los: de breuen al tpo dela
batalla / y esten los guerreros platicos / del pu yg su exp
tode la flecas

estos tres son vasallos del cacique

mexicano

valiente

valiente

valiente

valiente

tlacatecatl

tlacochcalcatl

huitznahuatl

ticociahuacatl

The Coyolxauhqui Stone

After the complete destruction of the Pre-Columbian city during the siege of 1521, all knowledge of Tenochtitlán's central religious precinct remained largely conjectural. The belief that the Great Temple might lay below Mexico City's contemporary *zócalo* or city center was seemingly confirmed in 1790 with the discovery of the monolithic sculptures known as the Calendar Stone (see page 116) and the Statue of Coatlique, the legendary mother of Huitzilopochtli. Colonial writings and diagrams appeared to indicate that the base of the Great Temple was approximately 300 feet square with four to five stepped levels rising to as much as 180 feet in height. Staircases were constructed on the west side that ended before the two shrines constructed at the summit. However, it was only recently that systematic archaeological excavation would either confirm or deny what the Spanish invaders had actually witnessed.

Then on February 21, 1978, Mexico City electrical workers were excavating a trench six feet below the street level to the northwest of the cathedral when they encountered a monolithic carved stone block. Archaeologists were immediately called to the scene to salvage what turned out to be an stone disk, eleven foot in diameter, carved with a relief in human form. Recognizing the golden bells on her cheeks, salvage archaeologists identified the image as a moon goddess known as Coyolxauhqui, "She Who is Adorned with Bells."

According to legend the goddess threatened the Aztec patron god Huitzilopochtli and he killed her. Careful examination of the Coyolxauhqui stone led the National Institute's director of excavations Eduardo Matos Moctezuma to conclude that the monument was "in situ," meaning it had never been seen by the Spaniards, much less smashed and reburied like so many other carvings. Remembering that Coyoxauhqui's body was said to have come to rest at the foot of a mountain, the archaeologists began to surmise that Coatepec, which is to say its incarnation as Tenochtitlán's Great Temple itself, might lay very nearby. Soon the archaeologists discovered parts of a grand staircase and then the massive stone serpent heads, literally signifying Coatepec, surrounding the base of the pyramid. The Great Temple had been found by decoding a 1000-year old legend. (John Pohl)

Michoacán, meaning "Place of the Fishes," constituted the center of the Tarascan empire of over one million people ruled by an hereditary lord whose capital was located at Tzintzuntzan on Lake Patzcuaro. Although Axayacatl had mobilized an army of over 20,000 men he soon encountered a formidable Tarascan army nearly twice that size. Apprehensive but not deterred, Axayacatl directed his troops to attack. The battle raged throughout the day and well into the night. By the next morning, with the best of his shock troops dead or severely wounded, Axayacatl was forced to make a fighting retreat, barely reaching Tenochtitlán with less than a fifth of his army still alive. The Sun Stone did not receive its promised tribute of hearts and blood, and the defeat sent shock waves throughout the empire. Before long many city-states were rising in armed revolt in order to exploit the chaotic situation. By 1481, Axayacatl died. He was succeeded by Tizoc, who ruled briefly but ineffectually. Many suspect that he was even assassinated by members of his own court.

In 1486, the throne passed to Tizoc's younger brother, Ahuitzotl, who proved himself to be an outstanding military commander. Ahuitzotl reorganized the army and soon regained much of the territory lost under the previous administrations. He then initiated a program of long-distance campaigning on an unprecedented scale. Bypassing the Tarascans, he succeeded in conquering much of coastal Guerrero, gaining free access to the strategic trade routes along the Pacific Coast through Acapulco. In 1497, he reconquered much of Oaxaca marching through Tehuantepec into Chiapas as far east as the Guatemalan border. Fearing that he would outdistance his sources of supply, he then attempted to return but found that he had been betrayed by the Zapotecs. Only when he had agreed to an unprecedented royal marriage between the Zapotec king Cocijoeza and one of his daughters, as well as ceding governorship over the newly conquered province of the Soconusco, was peace finally resolved. Nevertheless the empire reached its apogee under Ahuitzotl, dominating as many as 25 million people throughout the Mexican highlands.

With the accession of Motecuhzoma II in about 1503, the empire reached its height. A competent general, Motecuhzoma put down rebellions in the provinces, and conquered new ones. The only parts of the country that were able to resist Aztec rule were the powerful Tarascan empire of the west, in modern Jalisco and Michoacán, and the small, militant state of Tlaxcala in the east. The Aztecs tended to leave the Tarascans alone, because the Tarascan Empire was powerful enough to fight it to a standstill and inflict severe damage. However, a state of cold war existed with Tlaxcala and its allies, and frequently it broke into open fighting. When enemy prisoners were captured, they were offered up as sacrifices to the Aztec gods. The same happened to Aztec soldiers who were taken by their enemies. In either case, the victims were considered beloved of the gods, and, it was believed, would go directly to paradise. After one defeat, Motecuhzoma was informed of the sacrifice of Aztec prisoners by the victorious people of Huexotzinco. "For this fate we have been born," he observed, "for this we go into battle, and death in this manner is fortunate. That is the blessed death that our ancestors extolled."

PART TWO

WARRING SIDES

THE CONQUISTADORES

Introduction

In his pioneering *History of Mexico*, Hubert Howe Bancroft described the 16th-century Conquistador as being "of different material from the soldier of the present day," stating:

> He was not a mere machine; he was a great dealer in destiny. He would willingly adventure his life. If he lost, it was well; if he won, it was better. A hundred did lose where one gained, and this each might have known to be the risk had he taken the trouble to make a computation. His life was but one continuous game of hazard; but, if successful, he expected wealth and glory as a just reward.

In short, he was not a soldier in the conventional sense. Although many of those who accompanied Cortés did have formal military backgrounds in the Italian campaigns and elsewhere, they were essentially a company of adventurers. They paid their own way, often contributing to the overall cost of the expedition, and many had to take out loans in order to meet their expenses. They could incur further expenses in weaponry and mounts. Besides their food and equipment, all soldiers also paid what they considered exorbitant fees to the expedition surgeons who treated their wounds and tropical fevers, and to the apothecaries who provided the medicines. Their reward, if any, would be shares in the spoils of what they hoped would be a successful and lucrative expedition.

War and adventure were in their blood. A large percentage was not simply from Spain, but from Castile, the country that for centuries had been at the forefront of the wars against the Moors. Narrowing it down even further, the two greatest conquerors,

OPPOSITE
The Spaniards and Tlaxcalteca fight the Aztecs. (*Lienzo de Tlaxcala*, American Museum of Natural History)

ABOVE
Aztec soldiers. (Illustration by John Pohl from the *Codex Mendoza*)

Cortés of Mexico and his very distant cousin, Francisco Pizarro of Peru, were from the Castilian province of Extremadura. Literally translated as "Hard Extreme," Extremadura was also the extremity on the frontier between Christian Spain and Muslim Spain, and the battleground where the two forces so often clashed. A high, bleak plateau of windswept plains, large tracts of tough, gnarled oaks, and an overabundance of fortresses, it has always bred a hard, lonely, self-reliant people.

The terrain was only part of the force that forged the regional character. There was also a culture of war, a centuries-old crusading spirit against the infidel, a feeling of righteousness in the cause of Christianity. The end of the Moorish Wars in 1492 removed one infidel threat from the scene, but the void would be filled as the voyages of Christopher Columbus and his successors provided new ones. Extremadura was more than ready to provide the great captains of the Conquest, who then enlisted fellow Extremadurans to form the core of the invasion forces.

Organization and tactics

The Spanish army of the 16th century was unlike any other army in Europe at the time. It was forged through the *Reconquista*. Ferdinand's success was only achieved by arming the citizenry and forming them into militias, an act almost unthinkable in neighboring countries like France, where the elite class assured its very survival by restricting the right to bear arms and armor. After the defeat of the Moors, Ferdinand turned his attention to Aragón's claims to Naples and southern Italy, then threatened by a French invasion. The French had every reason to be frightened of the new Spanish army. Spanish halberdiers thought nothing of dragging the flower of nobility from their horses, allowing gunners to run their matchlocks up into their armor, literally blasting the helpless knights to pieces. The threat to an entire social order was very real and by 1500, the Spanish citizen-soldier had become the most efficient killer Europe had seen since the Roman legionaries.

Until the 15th century, the Spanish nobility was divided into numerous factions and tended to wage war defensively from the protection of castles. Campaigns were comparatively small in scale and usually entailed the raising of an army of heavily armored cavalry supported by archers whose principal function was to serve as a protective screen. The feudal organization of Spanish society demanded that virtually every nobleman perform as a fighting man, although little more training was required than to be able to sit astride a horse and handle a lance, sword, and shield with an elementary level of competence. Assembled only with difficulty, knights usually arrived in small parties and, because of the long-standing disputes between them, rarely fought in any coordinated tactical formations. With the emphasis placed on chivalrous notions of "courage," skill, tactics, or strategy had little role to play either. Once the enemy's position was sighted, nothing could restrain the knight; the shield was shifted forward, the lance dropped, spurs were put to the charger, and the armor-clad juggernaut thundered forward. Once the battle was over, the obligation of service was deemed complete and the survivors returned to their estates.

During the 15th century the situation began to change. Greater wealth, improved communications, and better transportation allowed rival princes to hire professional troops who were trained in the use of deadlier weapons like the crossbow, the gun, and the cannon. Many were the sons of an emerging middle class: the city-based merchants and skilled craftspeople who emphasized education in art, science, and technology. The dominance of heavy cavalry ended as new forms of combat relied on densely packed formations of infantrymen. At first the men were organized into units of 50, each under the command of a captain, but by 1500, these units were expanded to 200 men, anticipating the formations later known as *tercios* during the mid-16th century.

Successful as the Spanish foot soldiers had been in the rugged Andalusian mountains against the Moors, they encountered a very different kind of foe on the broad plains of Italy: the Swiss mercenary. The first Spanish army arrived in Italy in 1495 eager to test their skill against the French. At the battle of Seminara they found themselves facing a squadron of 800 Swiss pikemen. Superbly trained, brave, and brutal, they fought with 18ft-long spears in much the same way as the ancient Macedonian phalanx. The Swiss advanced rapidly in columns three deep, relying on the sheer impetus of their attack to drive their enemies off the field.

Beaten, but hardly defeated, the Spaniards were quick to adapt. At the battle of Cerignola in 1503, they coordinated equal numbers of gunners, pikemen, and

Many of the Conquistadores and their men came from Extremadura in western Spain including Cortés, Alvarado, and Pizarro. The region was characterized by broad stretches of open, rocky, grassland. More conducive to cattle-raising than farming, peasant youths would eventually take their chances in the army after droughts devastated the area in the early 1500s. Nowadays, the rocky terrain is used for raising livestock for the bullfighting industry. (Topfoto/The Image Works)

swordsmen. First the Spanish gunners shot massed volleys into the enemy's phalanx while the pikemen supplied a "hedgehog" defense. The horrifying gaps resulting from the concentrated fire were then exploited by the heavily armored swordsmen who dashed forth in dense packs to hack the Swiss to death, their own pikes being useless in such close-quarter combat. The combination was unbeatable and would serve the Spaniards equally well against the echelons of Aztec troops.

The extraordinary victories that the Spanish won in Italy were only possible under the command of an equally extraordinary commander. During the *Reconquista*, Ferdinand and Isabella wisely understood that military skills should take precedence over noble birth in the choice of commanders. As a result they regularly elevated commoners and rewarded them with both military titles and pure gold. One man in particular, Gonzalo Fernández de Córdoba, rose above the rest to become the kind of commander the Conquistadores most desired to emulate.

Córdoba was the younger son of a prosperous Castilian landowner who stood to inherit little of his father's estate. He first sought his fortune as a soldier fighting for princes engaged in petty disputes throughout the peninsula. His remarkable skill at both mobile and siege warfare during the Granada campaign brought him to the attention of Ferdinand and Isabella. His advancement at court was rapid and in 1495 he was appointed to command the Spanish expeditionary forces in Italy. Having learned his lesson well at Seminara, Córdoba was later credited with transforming the Spanish army into the fearsome fighting machine that emerged triumphant at Cerignola, and finally defeated the French at Garigliano in 1504, for which he was appointed viceroy of Naples.

Córdoba was known for his handsome and engaging manner, tremendous physical strength, and superb horsemanship. He displayed an elegant, luxurious personal style even on the battlefield. Being a deeply religious man who carried a small image of the Christ child on his person, he showed a natural mercy to his defeated enemies, frequently using his gentle manner to agree honorable terms rather than sacking and burning their cities as the rules of war dictated. Ruthless as the Conquistadores could be, they learned the advantages of diplomacy and coalition building from the man whom they venerated as the "Great Captain."

If Córdoba supplied the inspiration for leadership among the Conquistadores, it was Columbus who inspired the greatest technological innovation. Until the end of the 15th century, heavy ships known as *carracks* were employed for short-range commerce in European waters. Little was known about open-sea navigation and the craft tended to sail along coastlines to avoid sudden storms, enemies, and other hazards. Early *carracks* were square-rigged which gave them speed, but only under limited conditions in favorable winds. It was the adoption of the smaller Moorish-inspired *caravel* that allowed Columbus's men not only to sail swiftly across open sea, but to negotiate the narrow straits and shallow inland harbors that characterized the Caribbean islands and

A typical European square composed of gunners and pikemen for battlefield defense. During the battle of Otumba in 1521, the Aztecs surrounded Cortés and his men trying to induce them to panic. However, by forming up into dense squares, the Spaniards held off the Aztecs with matchlock and crossbow fire while the horse sallied forth to disrupt enemy troop coordination. (Detail from an engraving published by Théodore de Bry, 1591)

Sailors like these, drawn in 1529, were invaluable to Conquistador armies. They not only guided the ships through unknown waters in all sorts of formidable weather conditions, but served as engineers on land. Most were of Portuguese, Genoese, and Neapolitan descent. (Wieditz, 1927)

OPPOSITE LEFT

The stereotype of the Conquistador is of a mounted knight in full armor. Although painted by Indian people, who had considerable knowledge of events, such images are more likely derived from the religious pageants that were celebrated in Spanish colonial times to glorify the Conquistadores. For example, this horseman from the *Florentine Codex* is wearing a "caged" *burgonet*, a late 16th-century helmet style that was only displayed at special ceremonies of state and never worn in battle. (*Florentine Codex*, Book 12, Ch.22; American Museum of Natural History)

OPPOSITE RIGHT

The question of how to transport horses aboard ship was resolved with an ingenious system of hoists, harnesses, and slings to restrain the animals on deck. At 3,000 pesos each, horses were expensive and absolutely crucial to Conquistador campaigns. (Weiditz, 1927)

the Gulf of Mexico. Innovative combinations of both square and latine rigging enabled crews to actually sail into the wind, vastly improving their crafts' maneuverability, speed, and range. As legendary as the *caravel* became in the history of European exploration, it was even more effective as a military innovation. Such ships allowed the Spaniards to attack foreign territory on their own terms by comprising a moveable base of operations. As it was impossible for indigenous nations to determine where or when the Spaniards might land, they could not deploy their troops in any concentrated units to resist invasion. These ships could carry sufficient supplies to keep an entire army in the field for months or, with ready access to friendly ports, even years at a time.

However, it is true that men traveling aboard 16th-century ships equated the experience with six weeks of torture. They were confined in narrow holds below deck most of the time, where the stench of spoiled food, vomit, animals, and manure was overpowering. Yet somehow they managed by gambling, singing, dancing – anything that would keep their minds off their torment. They were fond of the ballads of great heroes like Charlemagne, Roland and especially El Cid, the 11th-century Iberian conqueror. Books were becoming more commonplace and might be read aloud on ships, to the delight of the men. The stories made such a profound impression on the Spaniards that they eventually named many lands they discovered after the fabled kingdoms of their novels: Amazon, California, and Patagonia. The name for the islands of the "Antilles" was even derived from the legend of the lost city of Atlantis itself. Some said that the sagas were nonsense, but there were legends of great epochs of gold and silver dating before the fall of Adam and Eve. Surely, these lost worlds had some basis in fact; it was just a question of going in search of them.

Dress and armor

Despite the fact that the Spaniards composed a national military force, there was no official uniform on the cusp of the 15th and 16th centuries. Soldiers were largely responsible for dressing themselves. Many would begin their careers wearing pull-over tunics, leggings, simple cloaks, and whatever else they could muster as farmers and laborers who had been formed into militia units. Later, wealth from plunder and exposure to the newly prosperous middle classes of merchants and tradesmen in cities throughout Italy, France, and the Holy Roman Empire fostered personal expression in general and a taste for fashion in particular. Like the fighting men of other nations, the Spaniards at first favored the soft fluid and elegant lines reflecting the idealization of the human form so important in Renaissance art, but this soon gave way to a conservative, even rigid appearance that contrasted drastically with the ruthless troops they so often opposed. The Swiss mercenaries, for example, were all colors, slashes, and puffs, with jaunty hats loaded with feathers.

Most clothing was made of wool, flax, or linen. Silk and fur were expensive and largely restricted to ornamental trim only affordable to officers. Shirts were cut full and gathered at first to a low neckline, but later into a small collar or frill, from which the ruff (so popular by the end of the 16th century) developed. Tight-fitting hose was worn over

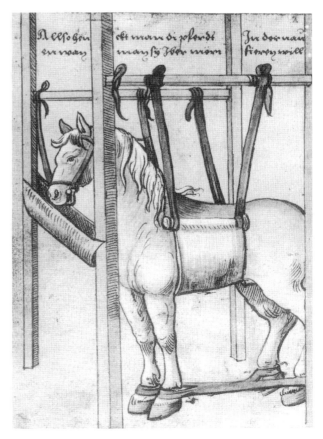

Conquistador clothing

In contrast to the Baroque stereotype of the morion-helmeted captain with the infamous thin goatee beard, most Conquistadores were actually Renaissance men who preferred Italian fashions. In the 1490s the clean-shaven look inspired by Classical art was favored (1). However, both Indian and Spanish sources refer to Cortés and his men as having beards, doubtless the result of their being continually engaged in campaign throughout 1519–21. There are many references to their "flat caps" which could be worn in any variety of forms, but stylish slashes to the brim were favored (2). By the 1540s short hair and trimmed beards became popular, as well as collared shirts and smaller feather bedecked hats often worn at a jaunty angle over the eye (3). The shirts were tucked into hose which were tied to a codpiece (4). The hose could then be secured by strings to the upper body garment, either the doublet (5) or the jerkin (6). At times the garments were tailored along such similar lines that it is difficult to distinguish them in contemporary art. Basically the jerkin was an outer garment worn over the doublet for added protection or warmth. At first such garments featured skirts reaching to the thigh but by the middle of the 16th century fashion trends had shifted to shorter forms.

Footwear was a necessity, but was very hard to come by. High-ranking men who also served as the cavalry wore boots (7). While the foot soldiers doubtless started with a basic leather shoe (8), they were soon worn out and the men resorted to wearing the indigenous style of sandal (9). (Adam Hook © Osprey Publishing Ltd)

the legs. The stockings were either pulled on separately, or sewn together and secured with ties to a cord, the shirt, or even the doublet.

The most common outer garments were the doublet and the jerkin. At times they were tailored along such similar lines that it is difficult to distinguish them in period artwork.

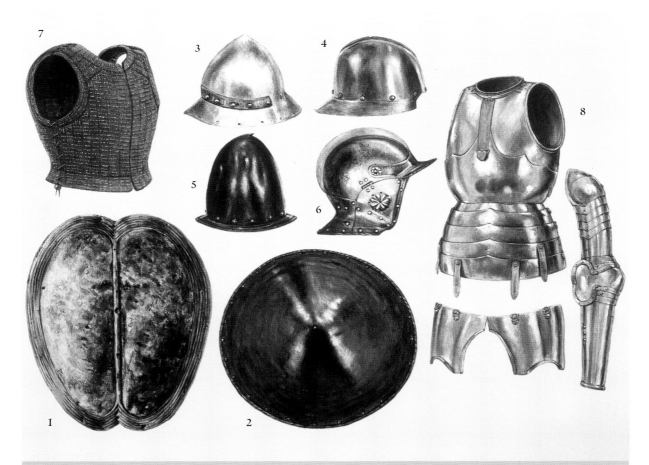

Conquistador armor

To what extent the Conquistadores employed protective armor depended on the campaign and the finances available. They used two types of shields. One, called an *adarga*, was originally of Moorish origin. It was frequently made of heavy ox hide embossed with decorative lines that followed the heart shape of the shield. Most were unpainted (1). The target was a 2ft-wide round of wood or metal with hoops on the back through one of which the arm was passed, while the other was grasped by the hand (2). The convex shape deflected direct thrusts against the body.

Helmets were largely variations on the war hat or *chapel de fer* (3) which had been easy to produce and provided good protection to the face and neck. The *celata* or *salade* was equally popular (4). By the early 16th century the domed *cabasset* (5)

was making its appearance, together with the *burgonet* which was especially popular among officers (6).

Body armor was very expensive but was crucial to cavalrymen who charged directly into deadly showers of Indian projectiles. The *brigandine* (7) was a padded linen sleeveless vest to which metal plates about 1in. wide and 2in. long were riveted. The plates were usually concealed by a covering of velvet or other fine material, but the rivets were left exposed and were sometimes even gilded. Steel body armor was also available, but was probably limited to the basic, including the breast and back plate, *tassets* for protection of the thighs, and *rerebraces* and *vambraces* for the arms (8). (Adam Hook © Osprey Publishing Ltd)

Originally, the doublet fitted close to the waist and was cut low and wide at the front to reveal the shirt. Its sleeves were slim to the wrist, but rose to become much fuller, even billowing at the shoulder, where they were either sewn or tied by points to the *scye*. By the beginning of the 16th century, the doublet was buttoned down the front from a high

As heavy armor began to prove unsuitable for the terrain and methods of combat in Mexico, Conquistadores sometimes carved a piece from their cuirasses, covered the sharp edges with rawhide and wore them over the chest area. Much lighter than the full breastplate, it allowed the soldier more freedom of movement, but was heavy enough to ward off most native weapons. This example is decorated with a cross. (Enrique E. Guerra collection)

collar and had a skirt which varied from very short to hip length. Sometimes the seams were concealed with the addition of padded rolls or wings. Sleeveless waistcoats, virtually identical in cut, were often worn underneath for additional warmth or as casual dress by men who could afford them. The early jerkin was also fitted to the waist but could be either high- or low-necked. It featured a pleated skirt reaching to just above the knee, but later it was shortened to above the hip. At first it was worn open to reveal the shirt, doublet, and codpiece but by the mid-16th century it was worn with a high-standing collar and could be buttoned from neck to waist. The skirts were no longer pleated, but still flared in varying lengths. Ultimately, the jerkin survived into the 17th century as the heavy cavalryman's buff coat, while the doublet became the basis for today's jacket.

Gowns were fashionable as overcoats. Initially worn long, they were subsequently shortened to the knee, very full with pleats at the back extending from a yoke. They were left open at the front and thrown back to reveal an ornamental lining which spread over the shoulders to a squared-off shape at the back.

Sometime after 1530, hose became separated into upper and lower stocks, the former becoming breeches, the latter stockings. With the shortening of the doublet, the breeches were revealed and took on a variety of lengths and shapes. They were basically constructed in three layers: a fitted base over which any padding was arranged, an inner

The *casque* helmet, which was hammered and riveted together, was much simpler and less ornate than the later *morion*, and would have been used by the ordinary soldier who had the means to buy it. (Enrique E. Guerra collection)

lining cut full, and an outer section less full, but slashed into long strips called panes that allowed the inner lining to show through.

The most popular head covering was the flat cap with its beret-shaped crown and narrow brim, worn either straight or turned up. Many were cut into sections and stiffened. Skull caps with small upturned brims were popular among sailors and soldiers alike.

Despite their appreciation for current European fashion, in reality Spanish soldiers had little recourse but to adopt the clothing of the nations in which they were campaigning. We know that they frequently received gifts of clothing from the Aztecs. The styles matching their own sensibilities would have included the *xicolli*, a short fringed jacket favored by priests, and a broad rectangular weaving called a *tilmatli* worn as a cape or poncho. Shoes and ankle boots would have been replaced with sandals.

The degree to which armor was employed by the Conquistadores is debatable. Very few of the participants who wrote of their combat experience discuss what type of protection they possessed or how much of it they actually wore. Either the Conquistadores used very little armor, or its employment was so commonplace as to be hardly worth mentioning. As effective as it had been for shock troops in Spain and Italy, armor's usefulness in the Caribbean was limited. It was insufferable to wear in the wet, insect-infested, tropical environment. Heavy, it radiated heat in excess of 200 degrees in

When besieged, the Spaniards attempted to drive off thick ranks of Aztec warriors by mounting gunners, crossbowmen, and other heavily armed soldiers in wheeled battle wagons constructed of thick timber. From the descriptions, they probably resembled this example depicted in a European woodcut and were pushed forward through narrow streets from behind. (Illustration by John Pohl)

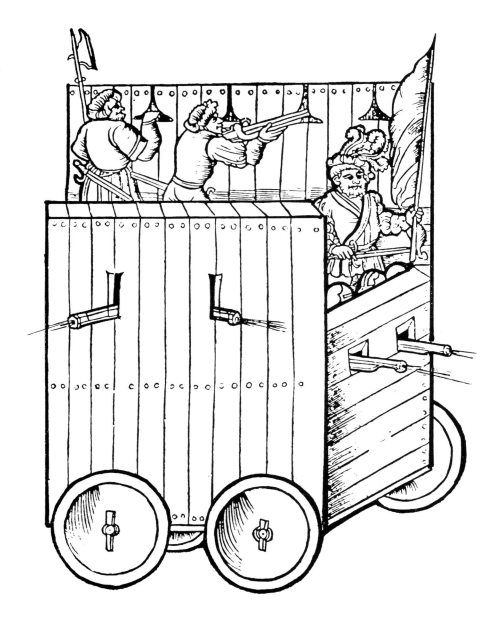

direct sunlight and had to be constantly cleaned or painted to protect it from rusting. Furthermore, it was expensive no matter how out of date it was, and campaign leaders working with the restrictive budgets imposed by their backers always opted for offensive weaponry over defensive protection.

Pictorial records of the opening phases of the Mexican campaign tend to suggest that Cortés's men wore very little armor. An Indian painting dating to within ten years of the event, known as the Tlaxcala Manuscript, depicts the Spaniards carrying swords, pikes, and lances, but wearing no armor upon their approach to Tlaxcala. Similarly, Bernal

Díaz speaks of a soldier wearing a "half gilt, but somewhat rusty helmet" as being a sight so unusual that it drew the attention of an Aztec ambassador. At a later date, however, Díaz refers to the Spanish horsemen in particular as being "well protected by armor," and the Aztecs themselves speak of men "completely encased in iron, as if turned to iron." The differences in the accounts suggest two possibilities; the armor was not ordinarily part of the personal equipment of the soldiers but rather, was packed with the supplies and distributed prior to a pitched battle, or else armor was simply acquired later in the campaign through resupply. The truth would probably incorporate something of both of these interpretations. It is also quite probable that the common soldiers, few of whom could afford European armor, adopted the quilted cotton armor of the Aztecs, which was light, allowed freedom of movement, and provided reasonable protection against the darts and sling stones of the natives.

Any armor available to the first expeditions under Columbus would have been limited to war hats and breastplates. Actual artifacts excavated in the southwestern United States indicate that there had been little change over a half-century later. The war hat or *chapel de fer* was an open helmet with a low crown and a broad round brim worn from the 12th to the 16th centuries. It was easily manufactured, transported, and distributed, yet despite its simplicity it was a practical defense for noble and commoner alike. During the 15th century another type of helmet evolved from the war hat, the *celata* or *salade*. At first, some versions of the war hat featured eye-slits in the brim allowing the soldier to pull the helmet down low over the forehead during combat without entirely impeding his forward vision. This simple modification was so effective that armorers began to lower the brim of the war hat entirely to enclose the lower part of the head. By 1450, both Spanish and Italian troops, however, began to favor a variation of the *celata* called a *barbute* that exposed the face.

The 16th century witnessed other modifications in the war hat, particularly the elevation of the crown and the narrowing of the brim. Such helmets first began to appear on Italian battlefields where they were called *cabassets* or "pears." Presumably the *cabasset* was introduced to Spain by returning veterans who would then have taken them to the Caribbean after 1500. It would actually be 30 to 40 years later before the fourth and most famous variation of the war hat began to appear. Called a *morion*, this distinctive crested helmet sported a graceful brim that swooped low over the ears and then rose to high peaks over the face and back of the head. Although it was never actually employed by the Conquistadores themselves, it eventually became so popular among Spanish troops serving throughout the empire, that its appearance was mythically transposed on to the notorious adventurers in later years.

Knights in full suits of armor had always been the most heavily armed of any military force in medieval Europe. During a charge they were frequently subjected to murderous barrages of missile fire before they could reach the enemy. Consequently, closed helmets would have been essential to their tactics, but to what extent the Conquistadores used them is unknown. The *armet* was the most common late 15th-century horseman's helmet.

It conformed to the shape of the head, but the weight was distributed over the shoulders by attachment to a broad gorget at the neck. Early examples had hinged cheek pieces that were joined at the chin under the visor. Later, a single moveable chin piece rotated into place on the same pivots as the visor itself. The drawback was that such equipment required a tremendous degree of workmanship by artisan-armorers, which was expensive. Totally enclosing the head, they were too hot to wear in the tropics and the systems of pivots and hinges would have been susceptible to rust, ultimately rendering them useless.

In the 16th century a new style of cavalry helmet began to appear called a *burgonet*. They were open helmets, with a brim projecting over the eyes and a standing comb. Nevertheless, they could be easily fitted with cheek plates, and when worn with a *buffe* or chin protector strapped around the base of the neck they supplied all the protection of the *armet* without the need for personal fitting or maintenance.

Like helmets, body armor was costly to purchase, ship, and maintain in the western hemisphere. During the Italian campaigns, it was normal for soldiers to strip armor from dead knights, but how much they sold off and how much they actually kept for personal use is difficult to evaluate. The most basic defense was chain mail which dated back to at least Roman times. It was produced by winding wire tightly around a metal rod and then cutting off rings that were riveted together. An ordinary shirt of mail could weigh anywhere between 15lb and 30lb depending on both the size of the rings and the garment. Some men may have been fortunate enough to acquire *brigandines*, protective vests made of plates of iron or steel riveted to a canvas garment and covered in velvet or other rich materials. Plate armor would have been Gothic in style, and infantrymen deployed as shock troops fought in breastplates. When available, cavalry were fitted out in three-quarter suits of plate armor that would ideally consist of breast and back plate, rerebraces, vambraces, taces, tassets, and cuisses.

In considering the quantity and quality of armor employed during the various Conquistador campaigns, one must take into account the practicality of the various forms of indigenous armor as well. For the most part, Indian weaponry tended to be limited to slings, bows, spear throwers, clubs, and swords edged with volcanic glass razors. The Aztec *ichcahuipilli* was the most basic form of defense against such an arsenal. Vests constructed of quilted cotton, they were designed to absorb the impact of a projectile rather than stop it and therefore functioned much like a European *aketon*. Finally, shields were essential for swordsmen and cavalry. The Spaniards tended to favor the round, convex target made of iron or wood and secured to the arm and hand by rings. A leather heart-shaped shield called an *adarga* was also very popular. It had originally been adopted from the Moors and would have been easy to fabricate in the Americas.

Offensive weaponry

The primary weapons of the Conquistadores included swords, lances, crossbows, matchlocks, and light artillery. Swords changed very little throughout the Middle Ages. They had a blade about 3ft long and were carried in a leather-covered wooden scabbard

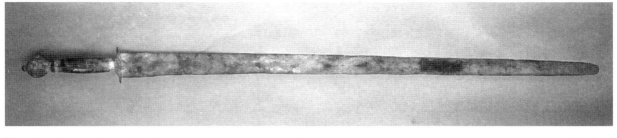

that hung vertically from a belt down the left leg. Most swords were sharpened on both edges, but usually blunted at the tip in order to slash at an opponent without it becoming entangled in surcoats and chain mail. Their hilts were relatively simple, featuring a sculpted pommel and a cross guard. By the 16th century new techniques for tempering metal, many adopted from the Moors, enabled Toledo craftsmen to forge swords called rapiers that were narrower, lighter, and sharper but sacrificed little in terms of strength and resiliency. Their needle-like tips were now intended to exploit gaps in armor and could even pierce chain mail. The hilt was enhanced by the addition of metal rings, many in fanciful combinations that not only added a sense of artistry to the weapon but in the hands of a skilled swordsman could be used to entangle the blade of an opponent and even disarm him. The longer rapier was suspended from a baldric, a wide belt hung over the right shoulder with its two ends attached to the scabbard in such a way that the sword hung diagonally across the lower back with the hilt over the left hip. The broadsword itself was never entirely abandoned and doubtless many Conquistadores continued to employ them, including a hefty 5½ft version that was wielded with both hands. Originally designed to break the pikes of their Swiss opponents, broadswords could also inflict devastating casualties on densely packed masses of lightly armed Indian troops. A variety of bills and halberds were available to the Conquistadores, as well as 12ft lances that were invaluable to cavalry squadrons who could disrupt even the largest formations of Indian armies with a series of coordinated, direct onslaughts as long as the terrain was flat and open. Doubling as pikes, lances could also be used by infantry to support units of swordsmen, crossbowmen and gunners alike.

The crossbow dated from at least the 3rd century AD, but they were not very powerful and tended to be employed for hunting in earlier times. Eventually, medieval craftsmen learned to make the weapon's 2ft-long arms stiffer by laminating various kinds of hardwoods, cane, horn, and bone together, but this made the weapon more difficult to cock. The solution was the use of a stirrup through which the foot was passed to secure

ABOVE TOP
This Castilian broadsword, discovered recently in Mexico City, may well be an actual relic of the Conquest. It was recovered from the site of an ancient canal on Cortés's line of retreat during *La Noche Triste*. (Enrique E. Guerra collection)

ABOVE
This remarkable, fully operational facsimile of a snapping matchlock by Dale Shinn is a copy of a weapon preserved in Basle dating to 1500. The barrel is made of bronze. The firing of a matchlock is a complex business. First the gunner blows on the lit match cord to make it burn hotter. Next, the match cord is secured in the jaw of the cocked serpentine. The priming pan is opened to expose the fine gunpowder that leads through the touch hole to the barrel and the main charge. The gun is carefully aimed. The gunner squeezes the button trigger with the fingers of his left hand, causing the serpentine to drop the hot match cord into the priming pan. In a flash of fire and smoke the priming powder is ignited along with the main charge, and the ball is propelled out of the barrel towards the target. (John Pohl)

the stock to the ground, while the string was drawn back with a crank attached to a cord and pulley system. By the 14th century the crossbow had become the essential weapon for all European armies. A 12in. bolt could actually pierce steel armor at close range. Furthermore, they were relatively easy to manufacture and needed less care than the matchlocks with which they were so often paired during the 15th century, a distinct advantage in the humid tropics of the Caribbean, Mexico, and Central America.

A common gunner might have credited the invention of his gun to an alchemist-monk named Black Berthold. According to a legend passed down by the old gunners, Berthold had been attempting to kill the spirit force that dwelled within mercury as the first step to making gold. First he heated the metal in a crucible, then he added charcoal, saltpeter, and finally sulfur. Needless to say, the exploding crucible nearly killed Berthold, but it also gave him the idea of using gunpowder to shoot projectiles. Whatever their true origin, guns were widely deployed on battlefields throughout Europe during the late Middle Ages. Little more than simple tubes of brass, bronze, or iron bound to straight staffs of wood, they rapidly gained popularity as they were fairly simple to make and required very little training to fire. By 1450, the prospect of an encounter with a peasant armed with a gun was a frightening proposition to a nobleman dressed in a full suit of armor. Being awkward to both aim and fire simultaneously, guns were notoriously inaccurate at first, but this situation was changed rapidly with the appearance of the matchlock by 1490.

Soldiers knew from experience with the crossbow that they could sight a gun and absorb its recoil better if they pressed the stock against the right shoulder to fire. It was just a question of devising a mechanism for automatically inserting the match into the

Conquistador weapons

Steel swords inflicted tremendous damage on Indian armies who had no experience with the metal before their encounters with Europeans. The most basic Conquistador weapon was the medieval-style sword. These were employed both as the 54in. two-handed variety (1) and the more common 32in. form (2). Later, changing styles in fighting led to the use of fancy hilts with intertwined rings and narrowing blades that would anticipate the rapier (3). The sword was supported by a very long belt to provide balanced suspension: when the extra length was wrapped around the body the second time, both hips then support the weight of the sword (4).

Lances (5) were made of ash wood and ranged in length, but most were probably about 12ft long. The heads were probably about 8in., the leaf shape inflicting especially gruesome wounds.

Halberds were generally about 6ft in length, but could range much longer (6). They consisted of an axe blade with a peak or point opposite it and a long spike or blade on the end. They were adopted from the Swiss who employed halberdiers to exploit breaks in defensive formations of pikemen, but they were ideal for holding Aztec infantry at bay while the gunners and crossbowmen reloaded.

The first matchlocks were a vast improvement over the old hand cannon and they were light enough to be held against the gunner's chest and aimed. Heavier versions developed in the 16th century featured a curved stock to help deflect the recoil, perhaps inspiring the term arquebus or "hook gun." This example is over 4ft long and employed a lever originally derived from the crossbow for a trigger (7). The barrel could be positioned on a staff for added support.

Crossbows were not only formidable weapons equated with the matchlock in firepower, but they were more dependable in the tropics (8). The stronger composition bows of horn, bone, and wood necessitated the use of a crank or windlass (9) to draw back the string. The projectile or "bolt" (10) was usually about 12in. long with a short steel head capable of penetrating armor at close range.

The Conquistadores were largely dependent on the falconet for their artillery since there were no wheeled vehicles or beasts of burden capable of hauling the heavier cannon during the opening stages of the invasion (11). The lightweight breech-loading guns were ordinarily deployed on the rails of ships to repel attackers. (Adam Hook © Osprey Publishing Ltd)

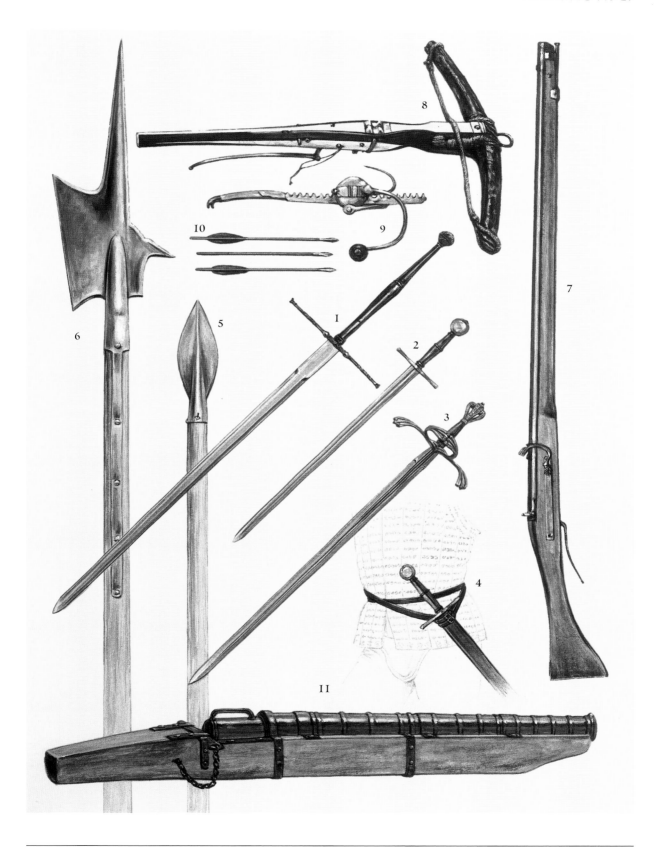

A wood block print illustrates an ingenious makeshift timber structure by which the Conquistadores could have deployed their falconets in land-based operations against the Aztecs. (John Pohl)

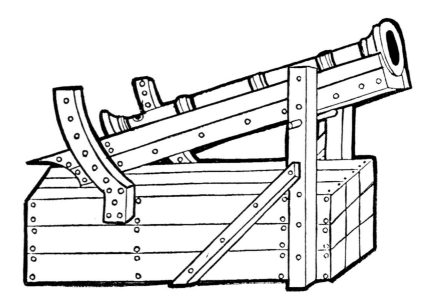

firing hole. The first matchlocks featured an S-shaped, pivot-mounted arm called a serpentine that gripped the match between its jaws. The gun was fired by pushing the lower part of the arm forward causing the upper part to rotate backward, thrusting the match into a priming chamber which in turn ignited the powder in the barrel. The development of trigger mechanisms later made the operation even simpler. At first a variety of different forms evolved, including an ingenious button trigger. During the 16th century a lever very similar to that on modern firearms was developed which acted upon the serpentine through a spring-mounted sear (from the French, *serrer*, to grip). Eventually such triggers were made smaller and were enclosed within a guard for greater safety from accidental discharge, while the serpentine was made to fall forward to allow the gunner to use his right hand for firing as well as to supply greater protection from the flash in the primer pan.

Until the standardization of Spain's arms industry under Charles V, guns were known by a variety of terms: *espingarda*, *arcabuz*, and *escopeta* were the most common. It was Córdoba who recognized the advantages of deploying large numbers of gunners as a force of fire on their own. Faced with the challenge of breaking the nearly impregnable squares of heavily armed Swiss pikemen that dominated Italian battlefields, a massed squadron of Spanish gunners could blast a hole in the formation from a safe distance of 150 yards, allowing the reserve of sword and buckler men to dash into the confused mass to finish the slaughter.

The first account of any major weaponry destined for the Caribbean is a 1495 request by Columbus for 200 breastplates, 100 matchlocks, and 100 crossbows. Obviously the armament for a squadron of 200 infantry, the order shows that the gun and the crossbow were used in equal measure in New World campaigns. Indigenous peoples possessed no cavalry, so pikes were less important. Rather Indian armies tended to fight in large dense formations of light infantry, and the primary danger for the Conquistadores was being surprised and overrun before they could bring their superior combinations of weaponry to bear on an opponent. Accounts written by Conquistadores such as Cortés, Díaz, Alvarado and others describe the challenges of keeping a massed enemy at a distance. Guns could inflict horrifying damage on vastly superior numbers, but they took a great deal of time to prepare, load and fire. Able to manipulate their weapons more rapidly, crossbowmen were ideal for providing cover for the gunners. Swordsmen could then deal with the enemy who broke through their ranks on an individual basis. Once an initial onslaught was stopped, artillery could be positioned to allow the Spaniards to keep an enemy at bay almost indefinitely.

The standard ordnance on most campaigns was a breech-loading cannon with a 2–3in. bore called the falconet. Usually mounted on the topside rails of ships to repel boarders, they were transported inland by the early Conquistadores who remounted them on makeshift carriages or even timber scaffolds. With ranges in excess of 2,000 yards, they packed a terrific force capable of killing five or more men at a time. The sound they produced seldom failed to terrify indigenous peoples who associated such weapons with the supernatural forces of thunder, lightning, and volcanic eruptions. During the conquest of Mexico heavier cannon were also employed. Known by such imaginative names as *pasabolante*, *culebrina*, and *lombarda*, scholars still debate their sizes and calibers. Cortés was known to have had four falconets and ten brass lombards when he landed in Veracruz in 1519. The falconets were subsequently lost during *La Noche Triste*. It seems that the lombards were deemed too heavy to maneuver very effectively and were probably deployed for the defense of his coastal fortress at Villa Rica until a proper system of transport could be arranged, after which they were applied with devastating effect against the city of Tenochtitlán in 1521.

Portrait of a conquistador: Bernal Díaz del Castillo

> Bernal Díaz del Castillo, citizen and magistrate of the most loyal city of Santiago de Guatemala, one of the first discoverers and conquerors of New Spain and its provinces...

With these words, written some 30 years after the Conquest, a crusty, vain, honest old veteran began one of the greatest war memoirs of all time. Bernal Díaz del Castillo's *True History of the Conquest of New Spain* is just that – a true history. Whatever flaws or slips of memory it might contain (and there are remarkably few), it is not only one of the most accurate accounts of the Conquest, but also of the Aztec Empire at the height of its glory. No subsequent work on the Conquest or on Aztec Mexico can be written without it.

Like most Spaniards in Cortés's original band, Díaz was a Castilian, born in Medina del Campo. The records of his early life are sketchy. The date of his birth is given as either 1492 or 1496. By his own account, he was the son of Francisco Díaz del Castillo, called

A Castilian stirrup of the Conquest period, cast from heavy iron filigree in the form of a cross. As much weapon as horse furniture, it could be slammed into the head of a foot soldier in close combat. (Enrique E. Guerra collection)

"*El galán*" (the gallant or the handsome), a *regidor* or magistrate, and member of a quasi-noble class of squires known as *hidalgos*, or "people of substance." This position, while not one of great wealth, at least allowed Bernal an above-average education that is reflected in the *True History*.

There are no authentic portraits, but Díaz claimed to have been nicknamed *El galán* like his father, and in his own case he most certainly meant "the handsome." He was said to have been a *bon vivant* who tended to live beyond his means, an excellent conversationalist, and highly opinionated. He was an opportunist, open to any new ideas by which he might benefit, and touchy on what he felt was his just due. He was also a linguist. While in Cuba he learned the local language, appears to have picked up a basic proficiency in Nahuatl in Mexico, and, after eventually settling in Guatemala, spoke the Cakchiquel language of his Indian retainers there.

Díaz's story was typical of most of the soldiers who joined Cortés, having first tried their luck elsewhere in the New World. He left Spain in 1514 as part of the entourage of Pedro Arias de Ávila, who was sent to rule over the newly conquered province of Darien (now known as Panama). Disputes broke out between the brutal, iron-fisted Arias and his son-in-law, Vasco Núñez de Balboa, resulting in Balboa's execution. That, together with illness and a series of revolts against Arias's rule, left Díaz disillusioned, and he departed

for the recently conquered island of Cuba, where the governor, Diego Velásquez, was his distant cousin.

By 1517, Díaz had spent three years in Panama and Cuba without accomplishing anything of importance. Determined to do better, he joined a group of Spaniards in the same situation, and together they took out loans and joined the expedition under Francisco Hernández de Córdoba. This first exposure to the North American mainland, while disappointing, convinced him that it held opportunities, and he subsequently joined Juan de Grijalva's expedition. By 1519, when the Cortés expedition was organizing, he was as close to being a seasoned expert on the Mexican coast as was possible in that era.

Díaz was a romantic, and can perhaps be forgiven for allowing a certain amount of romanticism to work its way into his reminiscences. He had, after all, known a world that no European had imagined, and that few would ever see. He was also influenced by *Amadís de Gaula*, a romantic novel written in medieval times and printed for the first time in 1508. It quickly became the most popular printed book in Spain, and most members of the Cortés expedition who were literate had read it. Díaz certainly had, because he compares the approach to the city of Mexico with "the enchantments that are told in the book of Amadís." Amadís also worked its way into his impressions of Doña

Perhaps dating to the late 1520s a manuscript preserved in the Benson Library at the University of Texas, Austin, may be the earliest indigenous portrayal of Cortés's army on the march to Tlaxcala by eyewitnesses. Note that the Spanish soldiers are wearing late medieval to early Renaissance dress and little or no armor (left). At center, Cortés is dressed in black receiving the Tlaxcalteca Confederacy (right). (Benson Library, Texas)

A European woodcut illustrating the painful extraction of an arrow from a chest wound. The Spaniards frequently survived such injuries, only to succumb to infection days later. (Illustration by John Pohl)

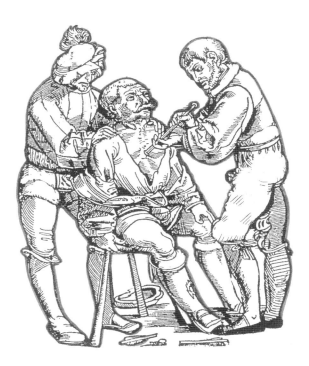

Marina because, writing in old age, he inadvertently drew parallels between her life and that of the fictional hero.

Like many soldiers of his era, he was both devout and worldly. He praised God for any outstanding turn of events in the Conquest. In battle, he believed that Christ had taken a personal interest in his survival, because otherwise he might not have lived to tell the tale. Yet for all his religious devotion, he was not above avarice and lust. Posted to guard Motecuhzoma, he asked a page to beg that Motecuhzoma "give me a beautiful Indian woman." Motecuhzoma summoned him, and said, "Bernal Díaz del Castillo, it has come to me that you have substantial garments and gold, and I will order that you be given today a fine lady-in-waiting; treat her well, for she is the daughter of a lord; and I will also give you gold and mantles." To that, Díaz knelt, kissed his hands, and asked God's protection over him. When this was translated, Motecuhzoma purportedly remarked, "It seems to me that Bernal Díaz is a noble man."

Díaz's writings convey an unabashed respect for Motecuhzoma. Whenever he encountered the emperor, he always respectfully removed his helmet. For his part, Motecuhzoma was impressed to learn that Díaz had served on the Córdoba and Grijalva expeditions, of which he was well aware. The one point of contention was the matter of sacrifices which Motecuhzoma was required to offer as high priest of the state religion. Cortés attempted to dissuade him, and when the emperor promised not to kill human beings, agreed to allow him to go to the temple. A detachment of four captains, 150 soldiers, and one of the chaplains, Father de la Merced, accompanied him. Despite his promises, Motecuhzoma killed several men and boys, and Díaz and the other guards could only turn away and pretend they had not seen it. On returning to their quarters, however, their feelings were assuaged rather easily by Motecuhzoma's gift of gold jewelry.

The surrender of the city brought disappointment. Much of the treasure had disappeared, lost in the fighting that began on *La Noche Triste*. Discouraged, Díaz joined an expedition led by Gonzalo Sandoval that ventured south into the Valley of Oaxaca, then across the Isthmus of Tehuantepec to Coatzacoalcos on the Gulf of Mexico, where Díaz was given three land grants with large numbers of Indian tributaries.

In 1524 Cortés decreed that all married soldiers had 18 months to bring their wives to the country, and bachelors must marry, or forfeit their property. Díaz appears to have complied by entering into a common-law arrangement with an Indian woman with whom he was living at the time. Always restless, however, he joined Cortés's ill-fated expedition to Honduras that same year, and in 1526 accompanied Pedro de Alvarado into Guatemala, passing through the region of the present city of Antigua, where ultimately he would make his home. Perhaps the thought already crossed his mind for, despite the fact that he was only in his late 20s or early 30s, illness and years of battle had left him feeling old and tired. Additionally, in the 1530s the king-emperor sent a cadre of bureaucrats to administer the new domains to the benefit of the Crown. Soldiers like Díaz, who had won the empire by their swords, lost their great landholdings at the stroke of a pen.

In 1539, armed with recommendations from Cortés and the viceroy, Antonio de Mendoza, Díaz went to Spain to defend his claims. Eventually he received compensation for the estates he had lost and confirmation of those he retained, and in 1541 he moved to Guatemala. There he received new estates and married Teresa Becerra de Durán, a well-to-do Spanish widow

The Spaniards were the first to employ what would later become known as "battleship diplomacy" in their dealings with foreign nations. Faced with increasing dissent among a faction of men loyal to Velásquez, Cortés had his ships scuttled shortly after arriving at Veracruz, thereby making the entire army solely dependent on his command. (Detail from an engraving published by Théodore de Bry, 1591)

whose father, Bartolomé Becerra, had been one of the conquerors of Guatemala, and whose first husband, Juan Durán, was an early settler. Thus, he settled to the life of a wealthy planter, participating in local affairs, raising his children by Teresa, and securing legacies for those he had with various Indian mistresses.

Díaz was keenly aware that he had participated in events that changed the world, and that he himself had witnessed a civilization that was gone forever. In the preface to the *True History* he wrote:

> That which I myself saw, and what I myself did in the fighting, as a good eye witness I will write, with the help of God, very simply, without twisting one part or another… I am more than eighty-four years old and have lost my sight and hearing, and by my efforts I have no other wealth to leave to my children and descendants, other than this my true and wonderful story…

This appears to have been the final of three prefaces he drafted, for he was already at work on his manuscript in the early 1550s, when he would have been in his late 50s or early 60s. The work itself occupied the rest of his very long life. For all his pleas of poverty, Díaz was a prominent citizen of Guatemala, an extensive landholder, and member of the ruling council. His public duties and business interests occupied much of his time, and he put aside the memoir for months at a time. He even abandoned the manuscript for a while, following the publication of Francisco López de Gómara's *Crónica de la Nueva España* in 1552, feeling that López de Gómara had rendered his own work redundant. Díaz was angered, however, that López de Gómara gave all the credit to Cortés when he believed the success of the Conquest was due to the efforts of ordinary soldiers such as himself. He resumed his work, completed it, then continued rewriting and refining it until his death in his late 80s, at the beginning of 1584.

Whatever Díaz's indignation at López de Gómara's hagiography, the figure of Cortés dominates the *True History*. Díaz is aware of his deviousness and self-interest, yet there is no question that he admires him. Throughout the narrative, Díaz refers to him as "Our Cortés" or "Our Captain," and was obviously prepared to follow him anywhere.

Despite its antiquity, *True History* is timeless. It is an old soldier's reminiscences, devoid of any theories, political causes, or petitions for honor, and has a ring to it that would be recognized by soldiers of any era. Bernal Díaz del Castillo would find himself among comrades at any veterans' gathering of the 21st century.

THE AZTEC WARRIORS

The Aztec army was one of the very few instances in the New World where Europeans encountered members of a formal, organized military establishment, rather than tribal warriors. A Spaniard known to history only as the "Anonymous Conquistador," wrote:

It is one of the most beautiful sights in the world to see them in their battle array because they keep formation wonderfully and are very handsome… Anyone facing them for the first time can be terrified by their screams and their ferocity. In warfare they are the most cruel people to be found, for they spare neither brothers, relatives, friends, nor women even if they are beautiful; they kill them all and eat them. When they cannot take the enemy plunder and booty with them, they burn everything.

By killing and eating, the Conquistador undoubtedly meant capturing victims for sacrifice. Taking captives for sacrifice was the great testimony to the warrior's prowess in battle. Although there was a hierarchy with a ranking system comparable to a modern army, the Aztec soldier was not a member of a large, monolithic force as is understood today. His loyalty was severally and variously tied to his ward or district in the city, the headman of that ward, the emperor, the state, and other interests. In this sense, he might be compared to the volunteer soldier of the Union Army during the American Civil War, who had divided loyalties to entities such as his county, state, and to the federal government.

The early years of a warrior

In Mexico, daily life was governed by religion. Soon after the birth of a child, the father would summon the *tonalpouqui*, or soothsayer. Using a folding book or codex, the *tonalpouqui* would determine the prophecy of the child's future. Pictographs were composed of one of 20 day signs and up to 13 numerals. There is some indication that if the actual birth date had a poor prophecy, the *tonalpouqui* could designate a more

ABOVE LEFT
Students arrive at the *telpochcalli* or young men's house. Note the father talking to a *cuahchic* about his son. (*Florentine Codex* Bk 3, Ch. 5, American Museum of Natural History)

ABOVE RIGHT
An enemy generally admitted defeat when the Aztec army succeeded in burning the temple of a town's principal god. Note the Huexotzincan warrior covering his mouth in astonishment as a warrior torches the temple. (*Florentine Codex* Bk 8, Ch. 17, American Museum of Natural History)

favorable time. In effect this became a way by which priests assigned life's work to each member of the *calpulli* from birth. *Matlactli cuauhtli*, or Ten Eagle, was the 75th day of the 260-day count of a sacred calendar. Given that day was so propitious, there were doubtless many Ten Eagles in Aztec society.

An Aztec child destined for a military life would have little to look forward to but a youthful life of toil. His education between the ages of three and fifteen was entrusted to his parents who taught him all that he should know of his *calpulli* (or town district) and the role that he should play in serving it. At first, he would spend years performing simple domestic tasks strengthening his body through heavy labor carrying wood, water, or supplies and food purchased in the market place at the center of the city. At seven he was trained to manage his family's boats and to fish on Lake Texcoco. When he wasn't participating in some ritual feast, he was encouraged to subsist on relatively meager amounts of food, being given only a half a cake of maize per meal at age three, a full cake at age five, and a cake and a half at age 12. This prepared him for his future when he might have to march for days without any food at all. Punishments for idleness were severe and ranged from beatings to stinging with Agave thorns or even having his face and eyes burned with the smoke of roasted chili peppers.

The *Codex Mendoza* includes an excellent pictorial account of the lives of soldiers. The soldier on the left is armed with a *tepoztopilli*, something like a halberd. He carries a *cacaxtli*, or carrying frame, to which are bound additional supplies together with cane for making arrow shafts. (*Codex Mendoza*, Bodleian Library, Oxford)

Depending on family background and social status, boys were sent to one of two schools, the *telpochcalli* for commoners, or the *calmecac* for the children of nobles. These schools offered training in a variety of fields, including the military. The sons of nobles and soldiers were most likely to take up the warrior's profession themselves. When a boy arrived, his parents took him before the *telpochtlato* or "ruler" of the school and the sacred image of the god of the youths:

A basalt statue of the Aztec god Quetzalcoatl whose name meant "feathered serpent." (Roger Viollet/Topfoto)

Here our lord has placed him. Here you understand, you are notified that our lord has given a jewel, a precious feather, a child has arrived. In your laps, in the cradle of your arms we place him. And now we dedicate him to the lord, shadow, wind, Tezcatlipoca and pray that he will sustain him. We leave him to become a young warrior. He will live here in the house of penance where the eagle warrior and the jaguar warrior are born. (Sahagún, *Florentine Codex*, Book 3: 51–53)

In addition to his daily chores both at home and at the school, a boy would work in a team of boys in public works particularly the cleaning and repairing of the aqueducts, canals, and causeways that criss-crossed the city and provided vital links for transportation.

Tenochtitlán had developed on a small island off the western shore of Lake Texcoco. Here the forefathers had managed to survive by learning to fish and harvest a seasonal bounty of wild birds and other foodstuffs. Later the men of each *calpulli* organized themselves into teams and began to construct artificial fields called *chinampas* by cutting drainage canals through the marshes. Separate plots were staked off with poles lashed together with vines and filled with alternating layers of decomposing plants and fertile mud from the lake bed. Willow trees were then planted so that their roots could anchor each new plot to the lake bottom thereby inhibiting erosion. The *chinampas* were then fertilized by recycling the human waste from the community itself. This ingenious system of reclamation soon allowed the Mexica to grow as many as three crops of corn per year and to quadruple the island's land mass. The lake surrounding the island had supplied a natural barrier to enemy attack, a strategic advantage when the Mexica began to hire themselves out as mercenaries during the dry season. As wealth and prosperity increased, however, so did the need for a more permanent line of essential supply from trade with the kingdoms surrounding Lake Texcoco. An agreement was first arranged with Chapultepec to construct an aqueduct that brought fresh water to the city from where it had once had to be transported by canoe. Soon additional causeways were constructed that linked Tenochtitlán to both the northern and southern shores, but the Mexica had the forethought to incorporate a system of bridges that could be removed during periods of threat from outside attack. In this way the city could be transformed into a nearly impregnable fortress.

By the middle of the 15th century, the Mexica were growing rich in war tribute and the emerging elite sought to increase their rank and prestige by redistributing this new-found wealth through a system of annual feasts dedicated to the pantheon of gods. In order to magnify the importance of these festivities they began to direct the construction

Cuextecatl soldier, AD 1500

Soldiers who succeeded in capturing two enemies were awarded a uniform consisting of a body suit called a *tlahuiztli*, a tall conical cap called a *copilli*, and a shield marked with black designs described as "hawk scratches." The *tlahuiztli* was made of sewn cotton. Red, yellow, blue or green feathers were meticulously stitched to the cloth in the workshops of conquered city-states and sent to Tenochtitlán each year as tribute. The design of the cap (1) was adopted as a trophy emblem from the Huaxtecs of coastal Veracruz following Motecuhzoma Ilhuicamina's subjugation of the region between 1469 and 1481. The frame was constructed of cane. The Huaxtec area held a particular fascination for the Aztecs because it was rich in cotton. The goddess of spinners and weavers was called Tlazolteotl. For this reason the soldiers thought it appropriate to wear hanks of un-spun cotton through their ear spools (2) as well as the *yacameztli* or "nose moon" in gold (3) in honor of her role as a patron of the moon. In addition to the battle suit, the emperor rewarded soldiers with a distinctive cape called a *tilmatli* that allowed them to display their rank when off-duty as well (4). The loin cloth or *maxtlatl* (5) was hand woven and embroidered by the soldier's own wife or mother (5a). The method of wrapping the cloth around the body and tying the ends at the front was a distinctive fashion for Aztec men (5b). The knot was then passed through an opening in the *tlahuiztli*. Sandals (6) were woven with thick grass soles to which were stitched a cotton strip to support the ankle and ties. Traditionally uniforms were burned upon the pyres of their owners at death, but during Spanish Colonial times the Indian descendants of great warriors continued to preserve the garments as valued objects of inheritance and even entitlement. (Adam Hook © Osprey Publishing Ltd)

of enormous temple and plaza precincts. The complexes served something like theaters for the reenactment of religious dramas that bound the families of each *calpulli* together both ritually and socially and it was here that both the priestly *calmecac* for the high born and the warrior *telpochcalli* for the commoner were located.

Many of the *telpochcalli* masters were hardly older than the boys. It was their job to watch and observe the new boys, looking out for those who were not only physically fit but showed respect and good judgment as well. Doubtless they intimidated the youths with insults and physical bullying as drill instructors have done in every army since time immemorial, but it was essential to determine who would thrive in the life and death situations of real combat. If a boy persevered he would be promoted to become a master of youths and perhaps later in life even a *telpochtlato*, a man responsible for training an entire generation of seasoned warriors, upon which the empire depended for its survival. Drunkenness in general was forbidden in Aztec society and even punished with death. The most enjoyment a *telpochcalli* student might hope for throughout his spartan life was the right to keep a mistress if he could afford one.

Aztec boys living at the *telpochcalli* had little time for the academic studies and religious exercises that were so important to the training of the children of prominent families that had been sent to the *calmecac*. Everything was done strictly to prepare them for war and back-breaking labor was the means by which a boy would be tested throughout each and every day. The only relaxation he could enjoy was during the evenings spent singing and dancing, exercises that would bond the boys of each *calpulli* together spiritually as well as training them in the agility and coordination that would become so essential to both hand-to-hand combat and troop movement. Many of the songs were dedicated to the exploits of the gods, culture heroes, or warriors of the *calpulli* who had accomplished great feats of heroism. Tezcatlipoca, the school's patron, was believed to embody the most admirable values of a soldier. The god was bold and daring. He had used cunning to outwit his rival at Tollan, Quetzalcoatl, shaming him before his people and banishing him from his realm. But there was a dark side to Tezcatlipoca, even a sense of fatalism, for he was known to deceive his followers, instilling in them false pride only to withdraw his divine protection when they needed it most and watch as they destroyed themselves. It was surely no coincidence then that Quetzalcoatl was venerated as the patron god of the *calmecac* where the virtuous ideals of the elite were emphasized through scholastic and devotional learning.

Training

Boys were introduced to the actual violence of war through the principal religious festivals that were held throughout the year in Tenochtitlán's central ceremonial precinct. Towards the end of the dry season between February and April, festivals dedicated to both the storm god, Tlaloc, and the war god, Xipe Totec, were celebrated in Tenochtitlán's main ceremonial center before the Great Temple. Here thousands of people would gather to celebrate the conclusion of the "war time" and the onset of the planting season with feasting, dancing, and singing. The featured events, however, were the staged battles during which high-ranking enemies captured during the previous campaign season fought for their lives in bloody gladiatorial combats against heavily armed opponents. At other times the students of both the *calmecac* and the *telpochcalli* were encouraged to participate in mock combats competing as teams against one another for food, gifts, and other rewards. Veteran warriors of different ranks and specialization taught the youths to handle all of the basic weapons such as slings, bows, arrows, and spears. The more promising students were soon advanced to training in the use of the sword and shield.

No less essential to developing agility, speed, and endurance was the ball game, a sport dating to at least the second millennium BC. Once they had discovered the resilient properties of rubber, Mesoamericans created a variety of different versions of the game with competitions involving anywhere between one and ten men on a side. The game is still played in parts of Mexico today. The object is intensely territorial with two teams volleying the ball back and forth until one side is no longer able to keep it in the air. At the point where the ball hits the ground, referees mark the territory that is lost to the opposition. The match is forfeit when one team is driven so far into the end zone that they can no longer effectively maneuver. By late Aztec times the games bordered on social mania with elite and peasants alike wagering their entire fortunes on the outcome of a single game. In some cases matches were actually played as an adjunct to war. Axayacatl provoked the king of Xochimilco into playing a ball game and wagered the tribute of a number of kingdoms around Lake Texcoco. When his opponent won the match, Axayacatl attacked and executed him.

If a boy proved himself physically and mentally to his school masters he would be recommended for recruitment. During the late 15th century and early 16th century, there would have been no shortage of opportunities to prove himself on the battlefield. A standard first assignment might be to serve as a porter to an older boy from the *calmecac* who had recently succeeded in capturing an enemy. Achievement in the Aztec imperial army was dependent upon the number of captives that one took in battle and the status that each captive held among his own people. The Huaxtecs were frowned upon as relatively unworthy opponents and so those who captured them were not granted particularly rich rewards. A warrior who succeeded in capturing one of the Tlaxcalteca on the other hand was highly revered.

As well as wars of conquest and subjugation, the Aztec engaged in events known as "flower wars." These wars were fought by prearrangement with a selected enemy for the sole purpose of providing the blood of captive warriors for the altars on the temples in the Aztec capital. Besides bringing in new sacrificial victims, it also gave practical combat experience to young warriors newly emerged from training. The location of the contests was ordinarily predetermined through regular diplomatic channels and generals from both sides served as referees. The arrangements made, the armies of Tenochtitlán and its allies would march on the enemy. Companies were organized to assure a suitable mixing of new recruits with seasoned veterans. Originally the battles were waged

Aztec battleline, AD 1500

Two *cuahchique* stand forward shouting insults and mocking the enemy in an effort to provoke the foolhardy to break ranks and attack the center of their main body. The Aztecs favored the deployment of troops in extended battlelines in their efforts to entrap their foes through double envelopment. The seemingly haphazard display of military pageantry is due to the fact that soldiers of differing ranks have been purposefully teamed up so that recruits can hone their skills in actual combat with the more experienced veterans. Having proven themselves competent fighters and eager to earn even greater rewards, the majority of

front-line soldiers are of *cuextecatl* rank. They are easily identifiable by the cone-shaped *copilli* headdress. Soldiers of the more advanced jaguar and *otomi* ranks have moved forward through the mass of raw recruits gathered at the rear to prepare for the shock of an impending attack. The magnificent standard rising up over the back of the battleline signals the arrival of a captain who will evaluate the likelihood of an attack and relay the message to the supreme commanders who would be observing the situation from an adjacent promontory. (Adam Hook © Osprey Publishing Ltd)

something along the lines of the European medieval mêlée. Emphasis was more on the display of prowess than the total defeat of the enemy. Every effort would be made to avoid killing enemy warriors in order that they could be captured and returned to the city as offerings to the gods. Fra Durán described one scene in 1487, in which 80,400 captives were sacrificed at the dedication of the Great Temple, the victims lined up on the causeways according to which allied army captured them. Furthermore, early Aztec politics was factional and any chance of escalating a flower war into full combat was to be avoided: this year's foe might very well become next year's ally. By the late 15th century, however, Ahuitzotl was becoming increasingly desperate to defeat the Tlaxcalteca and their allies so battles between the rival armies at that time were beginning to be waged as flower wars in name only.

Weaponry and protection

The weaponry with which Mexican boys were trained had much in common with ancient armies throughout the world; however, considering that they were essentially a primitive people, Mexican warriors were well armed for combat by the standards of the 16th century. The sons of farmers, the majority of the peasant population, would have been self-trained with the sling in order to supply the small game that thrived in the fields for the household dinner table. The weapon could be simply finger woven of *maguey* fiber, anywhere and at any time. A 5ft (1.52m) loop of cord was passed through a thong to hold the projectile in place. One end was wrapped around the three index fingers and the other was held between the forefinger and the thumb. Momentum was built up by swinging the loop over one's head four or more times and releasing the thumb at the point in the arc when the thong was oriented toward a target. Employed in actual combat, the sling was capable of propelling small oval stones specifically selected for their aerodynamics straight through a man's skull at a range in excess of 200 yards. A large shower of stones unleashed and smashing into an enemy simultaneously caused substantial casualties, and even heavily armored Europeans suffered serious injuries.

Being the original weapons of their Chichimec ancestors, boys were trained in the use of the bow and arrow and they practiced their skill in group hunts held in the surrounding mountains during the religious festival of Quecholli. Bows varied in length depending on their intended use, the longest being up to 5ft (1.52m). The best were made of hickory and ash wood, the strings were made from raw hide or animal tendons. Arrows were generally made from viburnum and straightened by repeated applications of moisture and heat. The "nock" or end of the shaft had two or three feathers attached to it to direct the arrow's flight. A cleft was made in the front end of the shaft and the point was glued with pitch adhesive and lashed into place. Points were made of a variety of chert or flint, but copper and obsidian were used as well. Three-pronged bone arrow points ordinarily used for bird hunting would have inflicted particularly vicious wounds. Bowmen and slingers were essentially equal in their capacity to wreak havoc on the enemy from a distance and were frequently paired in units. However, they were seldom employed as pivotal units for they were prone to be overrun and slaughtered at close range by more heavily armed opponents. They ordinarily took their places forward in order to shower the enemy with a barrage at the opening of an attack and then withdrew to the rear or flanks to lay down harassing fire as the troops began to engage in hand-to-hand combat. Unquestionably, Mesoamerica's most ancient weapon was the spear together with the spear thrower or *atlatl*. It now appears that the Clovis *atlatl* spear-point tradition of Paleo-Indian times was actually introduced by Solutrian peoples engaged in coastal umiak hunting for walrus and whale between northern Spain and North America

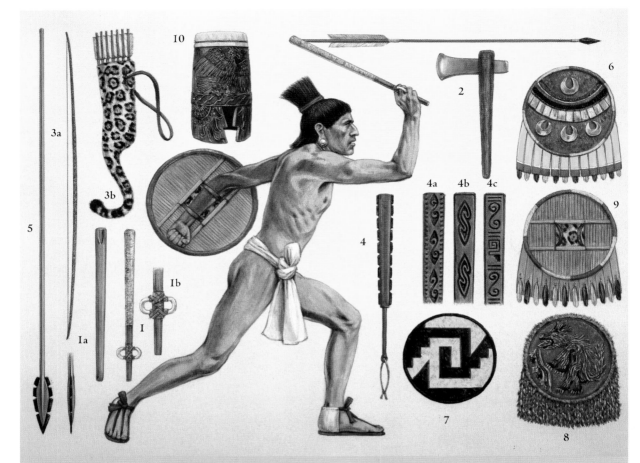

Aztec weaponry and equipment

Being largely an army of light infantry, the Aztecs maintained a relatively limited arsenal of offensive weapons in comparison to other armies throughout the world. The most ancient were the spear thrower (1) and the axe (2). Early spear throwers were composed of little more than a stick carved with a trough and a hook to secure the shaft (1a). More sophisticated versions featured special loops for the forefingers (1b). It became a most effective weapon for medium-range combat in the hands of noble warriors specially trained in its use. Being essential to agricultural production, most prehistoric farmers fought for their tribal chiefs with axes of ground stone. The widespread adoption of metallurgical technology from South America after AD 900 fostered the development of the more vicious cast copper axe head as a special weapon. The bow (3a) and arrows (3b) were adopted rather late as hunting tools in Mesoamerica, but in the hands of the Aztecs' Chichimec ancestors they soon became fundamental to laying down a barrage of deadly fire prior to an attack in warfare. The *macuahuitl* or sword (4) had been employed by earlier Mesoamerican civilizations. The Aztecs valued its particular ability to maim an enemy and were the first to employ it as a general issue

weapon. Many were carved or painted with intricate designs (4a–c).

While front-rank warriors engaged in slashing matches with the *macuahuitl*, troops armed with the *tepoztopilli* or halberd (5) harassed an enemy by thrusting or stabbing from the rear of the line. All Aztec soldiers were armed with shields. The few examples that survive in collections both in Mexico and Europe are all approximately 30in. (76cm) in diameter (6). Most are parade shields featuring remarkable heraldic designs in feathers such as the stepped fret (7) based on an example preserved in the Württembergisches Landesmuseum, Stuttgart, Germany, and a singing coyote (8) preserved in the Museum für Volkerkunde, Vienna, Austria (see page 70). The *cuexyo* shield (9) is reconstructed from eyewitness accounts which describe battle shields as being constructed of resilient woven cane or bamboo with heavy double cotton backing. Drums (10) were essential to coordinating the movements of large units closing in for the kill. The example illustrated is based on a *huehuetl* preserved in Mexico's National Museum of Anthropology. It is 3ft (0.91m) high and features a scene carved in relief depicting a dance of eagles and jaguars. (Adam Hook © Osprey Publishing Ltd)

around 16,000 BC. The subsequent advantage of using spear throwers on land was that they allowed coordinated groups of hunters to launch repeated debilitating attacks against large creatures like bison and mammoth without having to engage them physically. Aztec spear throwers ranged in size but most surviving examples are about 2ft (0.61m) in length. The thrower was grasped by slipping the first and second fingers through two loops either carved or lashed to the sides. The butt end of the spear was cradled into a depression that ran the length of one side. By casting the thrower forward with a whip-like motion the spear was launched against a target with as much as 20 times the force of arm strength alone. Many were magnificently carved from hard wood in a wide variety of ornamental designs. Serpents were especially favored and endowed the instrument with the spiritual qualities of a living being; and so they are sometimes described in legends. Despite its widespread use by the Teotihuacános, Mixtecs, Zapotecs, and Maya, there is some debate as to how much the average Aztec soldier relied on the *atlatl*. It appears to have taken considerable practice to master and was therefore considered more of an elite weapon. It is notable therefore that it appears most frequently in the hands of Aztec gods.

Clubs and axes were widely employed. Roundhead clubs called *cuauhololli* were carved of hard wood. They were fairly easy to produce and were especially favored by the Huaxtecs, Tarascans and other foreign peoples. Their intent was to knock a man unconscious until he could be hog-tied up and moved to the rear of the line. Axes were probably as old as the spear thrower. Utilitarian in their origin, they appear in early Olmec art dating to 1000 BC as war implements in the hands of paramount chiefs. Axes were produced either of ground stone or cast copper and wedged into the perforated aperture of a wooden handle. These heavy weapons appear to have been used in earlier times as a preferred elite weapon for closing in on an opponent following a spear fight with the *atlatl*. Their employment by later Aztec imperial troops, however, was probably not widespread.

By far the single most important weapon used by Aztec soldiers was the *macuahuitl*, a sword carved of wood with a blade edged on both sides by obsidian razor blades

A scene from the *Codex Mendoza*. On the right, a high ranker is shown marching with a shield ornamented with feathers and a pointed war stick called a *huitzoctli*. He is escorted by a youth of the *telpochcalli* carrying food and supplies for the two as well as his own weapons in a heavy woven basket. (*Codex Mendoza* 62r., Bodleian Library, Oxford)

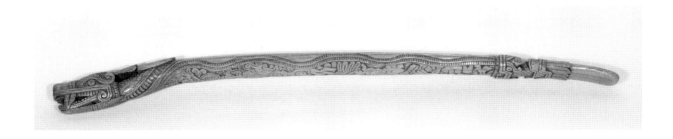

Aztec *atlatl* or spear-thrower. (Museo Nacional de Antropologia, Mexico)

attached with bitumen adhesive. Most examples were about 3½ft (1.06m) long but others were of such size that they had to be wielded with both hands. It appears infrequently if at all in Mesoamerica during earlier times when war was more of an elite activity, so we presume that its widespread use among the Aztecs emerged in response to the need to arm and train large armies of commoners as quickly and efficiently as possible. During the Conquest, one Spaniard described seeing "an Indian fighting against a mounted man, and the Indian gave the horse of his antagonist, such a blow in the breast that he opened it to the entrails, and it fell dead on the spot. And the same day I saw another Indian give another horse a blow to the neck that stretched it out dead at his feet." From such accounts we learn that the *macuahuitl* had little other purpose than to severely maim if not actually dismember the enemy. The Aztecs also employed a closely related weapon called a *tepoztopilli* as a thrusting spear similar to that used by the Zulus in the 19th century. But whereas the Zulu blade was steel, the Mexican weapon was carved from wood and featured a long, wide, wedge-shaped head fitted with a row of obsidian blades much like the *macuahuitl*. They varied in length from 3ft to 7ft (1.06–2.13m) in length. Younger warriors would have been assigned to wield such a weapon during their first battlefield experiences. It allowed them to stand at the rear of the line and shove or jab the weapon, harassing the enemy from a safe distance while the more experienced warriors fought in hand-to-hand combat at the front of the line.

The Aztecs did not have so much of a Stone Age culture as an obsidian culture. Obsidian is a volcanic glass formed by the rapid cooling and solidification of the silica-rich parts of extruded lava. Often thick vents of obsidian are subject to erosion, so that

concentrations of rolled and battered nodules appear in vast surface deposits, the largest of which were located around Tulancingo, 65 miles (105km) north-east of Tenochtitlán. Easily transported back to the city, the nodules were reduced to "cores" in the market places and distributed to hundreds of craft specialists who manufactured arrow points, knife blades, spear heads, and thousands of micro-blades used both for utilitarian and military purposes. Obsidian is a disposable technology, the antithesis of expensive and labor-intensive iron or steel. An obsidian worker can produce a blade in a matter of seconds, use it until it becomes dull or broken, and then simply strike a new blade to refit a weapon under virtually any kind of field conditions including combat itself.

The novel weaponry developed by the Aztecs fostered a need for equally ingenious forms of defense. For example, the vicious slashing and cutting that resulted from the *macuahuitl* necessitated the use of much larger shields than those used by earlier cultures. Circular shields called *chimalli* were generally about 30in. (76cm) in diameter. The strongest were constructed of fire-hardened cane or wooden rods interwoven with heavy cotton. They were further decorated with a lower fringe of feather, leather, or cloth strips to provide additional protection to the legs. Others were composed of solid wood sometimes sheathed in copper. Shields were lavishly painted or ornamented with featherwork in a wide variety of heraldic designs that demonstrated the prowess of the owner, the most popular being the *xicalcoliuhqui* and *cuexyo* designs.

There were various forms of head protection and even the standard warrior's hairstyle or *temilotl*, formed by gathering up the hair of the top of the head to form a broad top-knot, would have impeded any direct blow to the skull considerably. Protective caps or hats were also worn with certain forms of battle dress. Helmets took the form of eagles, jaguars, or other symbols that could designate rank or military order. Often they were made of wood and bone, heavily decorated with featherwork. When a military order had a large totemic animal, like a jaguar, wolf, or puma, the actual head of the animal might be mounted over a frame of wood or a quilted cotton liner, with the warrior looking through the animal's mouth implying that the man was essentially one with his animal counterpart in religious belief. Besides being defensive, these war suits and helmets were designed for psychological impact, to terrify an enemy.

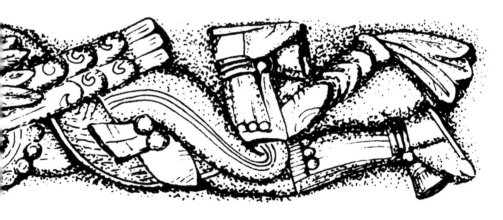

Detail showing the intricate carved and gilt design on the back of an *atlatl* or wooden spear-thrower. (Ann Ronan Picture Library/Heritage-Images)

Nearly all soldiers wore armor jackets of cotton quilting called *ichcahuipilli*. As the Spaniards learned shortly after reaching Hispañola, metal armor was impractical in the hot, humid regions of the Caribbean, Mexico, and Central America. The *ichcahuipilli* was something more akin to a bullet-proof vest in that it was not designed to stop the force of a projectile on impact but rather absorb it. It came in many forms. The open-sewn garment could be worn like a jacket and tied in front with laces or ribbons. The closed-sewn garment was a vest that was pulled on over the head. Appearances of the *ichcahuipilli* in pictographic books indicate that they were worn in a variety of lengths from the waist to the calf. Most were left natural but some were dyed in bright colors. Cotton quilted jackets were frequently worn under or incorporated into an elite garment called the *ehuatl*, a closed sewn tunic made of cotton ornamented with animal skin or feathers. The *ehuatl* was also distinguished by a skirt of leather or cloth strips and feathers that protected the thighs. Aztec emperors were known to have favored an *ehuatl* of red spoonbill feathers when they personally took to the field. Arm and wrist bands as well as greaves of wood, bark, and leather sometimes sheathed in metal were generally worn with the *ehuatl* for additional protection.

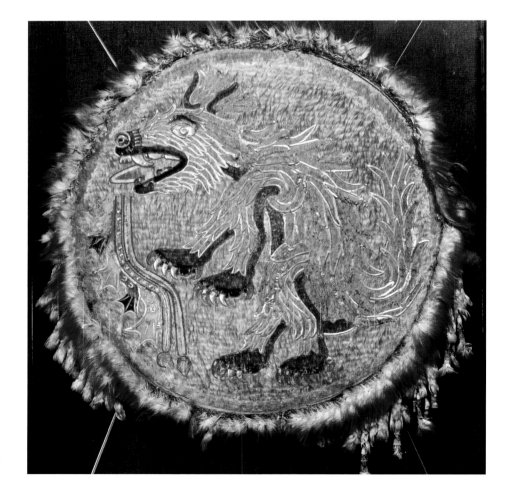

An Aztec featherwork parade shield depicting a coyote. The scroll emitting from the animal's mouth is meant to indicate speech or song. Intricate art works of this kind were presented to Cortés as royal gifts. (Topfoto)

Aztec helmets and armor

Nearly all warriors were issued with some form of the
ichcahuipilli (1 and 2). The most basic form of this cotton
quilted armor was a pull-over shirt. It was always worn under
both the *tlahuiztli* and the *ehuatl* and gave the soldier a very
muscular appearance. Other examples appearing in
pictographic histories suggest that it was also worn as a tunic
or jacket by itself among high-ranking lords. Many were dyed
in vibrant hues of red and blue. The *ichcahuipilli* was perfectly
adapted to the hot humid climate that pervades much of
Mexico. The theory behind its use was more like a
contemporary bullet-proof vest for absorbing the blow of a
weapon rather than attempting to stop it like medieval metal
armor. Helmets were carved of hardwoods like mahogany.
They were lined with a heavy cotton cap and tied securely
under the chin with cloth or leather ribbons. Those issued as
awards to soldiers were limited almost exclusively to the jaguar
(3), coyote (4), and *tzitzimitl* (5) or "demon of vengeance"
styles. However, high-ranking nobility could commission
helmets for themselves in all sorts of fanciful heraldic forms
with eagles, parrots, vultures, monkeys, bears, wolves, and
crocodiles being especially popular. (Adam Hook © Osprey
Publishing Ltd)

Dress and distinction

The Spaniards must have been bewildered by the sheer variety of battledress in an Aztec
army. These ritual garments actually composed the basis for a sophisticated system of
uniform distinctions. In most cultures, uniforms are used to differentiate units, but in the
Aztec army, uniforms served to differentiate men with different levels of military
experience within the same unit. Nearly everyone in a *xiquipilli* or regiment was closely
related because troops were recruited within the same *calpulli* neighborhood. Unit

A simple cotton quilted armor jacket was the most basic Aztec warrior garment. Worn under the *tlahuiztil* or the *ehuatl*, it gave the soldier a formidably stout appearance. We know that Cortés had quilted armor in this style made up in Cuba for his troops. (Reconstruction by John Pohl)

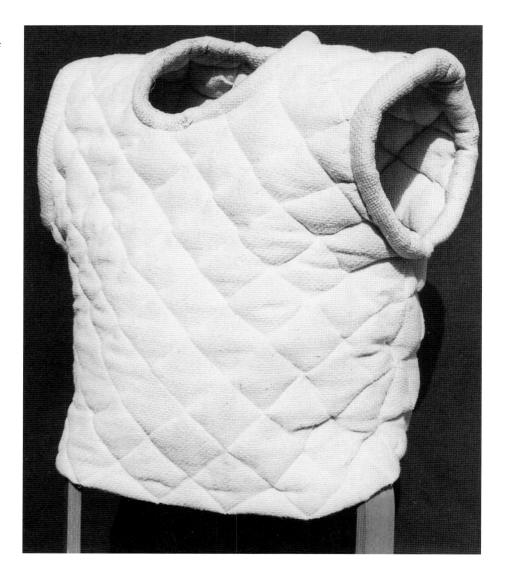

morale and mutual responsibilities were therefore dependent on family ties and it was the sworn duty of the veterans to look out for the recruits. The display of their lavish uniforms must have been a tremendous symbol of pride and encouragement to the youths who fought alongside them. When a youth joined the army, he had little more than a breech clout called a *maxtlatl*, sandals, and a short home-woven cape. The recruits would be taught from a pictographic book what each uniform was called, how it was constructed, and what it signified.

Rank distinctions in uniform between warriors depended upon how many captives each individual had taken. A soldier trained in the *telpochcalli* who had captured two of the enemy was entitled to wear the *cuextecatl*, a trophy uniform derived from the military dress of the Huaxtecs in commemoration of their defeat under Motecuhzoma I. The outfit consisted of a tight-fitting body suit called a *tlahuiztli*, that was woven of cotton and to which were sewn red, yellow, blue, or green feathers. A conical hat in matching color was worn as well. A soldier who succeeded in capturing three of the enemy was awarded a long *ichcahuipilli* together with a back ornament shaped as a butterfly. A soldier who succeeded in capturing four of the enemy was awarded a jaguar suit and helmet, and those who captured five of the enemy were awarded a green feather *tlahuiztli* and a back ornament called the *xopilli* or "claw." Accomplished soldiers who decided to become "lifers" were given a choice in promotion to a command position, or transfer to a troop of *cuahchique*, the "berserkers" of the Aztec imperial army.

The priests of the *calmecac* were similarly rewarded. When attending to their duties at the temples, priests were sworn to poverty and required to wear a *xicolli*, a simple unadorned cotton jacket that tied at the front. On the battlefield they were rewarded with garments that were every bit as lavish as the warriors of the *telpochcalli*. Those who had captured two of the enemy were awarded a white *tlahuiztli* and a back ornament, in reality the ritual staff of the goddess Tlazolteotl. Three captives earned one the right to wear a green *tlahuiztli* and a *pamitl* or flag painted with red and white stripes topped by a panache of priceless green quetzal feathers. Priests who had captured four of the enemy were awarded a *cuextecatl* in black ornamented with white circles representing stars. A soldier who captured five of the enemy wore a red *tlahuiztli* with a back ornament consisting of a great fan of scarlet macaw feathers called a *momoyactli*. Those lucky enough to achieve six captures were awarded coyote uniforms of yellow or red feathers and wooden helmets.

Military rank was also dependent upon social structure. The great speaker or *huey tlatoani* sat at the apex of Aztec society. By the 15th century the position had become tantamount to emperor. Below the *tlatoani* was a class of petty-kings or princes called *tetecuhtin* (*tecuhtli*, sing.) drawn from the *pipiltin* (*pilli*, sing.) or lords. However, ambitious commoners called *macehualtin* (*macehual*, sing.) could attain princely rank through achievement in warfare if they survived. This was accomplished by promotion through a series of officer ranks of which we know the names of at least 10. In addition there were four commanding officers (doubtless more restricted to the *pipiltin*) called the *tlacatecatl*, the *tlacochcalcatl*, the *huitzinahuatl*, and the *ticocyahuacatl*. Those who were promoted to the rank of captain and higher were awarded lavish uniforms equal to their high status, the most distinctive element being the large feather back ornaments that enabled them to be easily seen by their men as they walked up and down the back of the line shouting out their commands. Perhaps the most unusual outfit was that of the *Tlacochcalcatl* or Keeper of the House of Darts. These commanders were often close relatives of the emperor; in fact Itzcoatl and Motecuhzoma had served as *Tlacochcalcatl* before they were promoted to *huey tlatoani*. The uniform included a frightening helmet that represented a *tzitzimitl* or demon that was believed to take vicious revenge on all enemies.

When not wearing their battlefield gear, soldiers and officers alike were also entitled to wear a distinctive cloak called a *tilmatli*. The capes ranged in size from 4ft to 6ft (1.22–1.83m) in length and were customarily tied at the right shoulder and allowed to

Reconstruction of a hefty 5ft (1.42m) long version of the *macauhuitl*. The weapon was secured to the wrist with a slip knot. The effectiveness of the sword was dependent upon razor-sharp blades of obsidian struck from the platform of a prepared core. (Reconstruction by John Pohl)

Examples of tribute paid to Mexico by its vassals. The highest percentage of warrior outfits demanded by the Aztec empire in tribute were the Huaxtec and jaguar-style uniforms. The jaguar uniform is shown here on the lower right. Also shown are a *tlacatecatl* captain's outfit with the *quaxolotl* back device (top left uniform) and a *tlacochcalcatl* captain's outfit with a *tzizimitl* demon helmet on the lower left. The bottom two shields are of the *cuexyo* design. The feather design was created using an adhesive, originally derived from plants of the orchid family. The strips of leather hanging from the bottom rim were designed to protect the legs. Reconstructions have shown that the proportion of these shields to the human body was larger than portrayed here. The top left of the four shields has the *xicalcoliuhqui* or *greca* design. These shields were among the most common shields awarded to Aztec soldiers. (folio 20r., *Codex Mendoza*, Bodleian Library, Oxford)

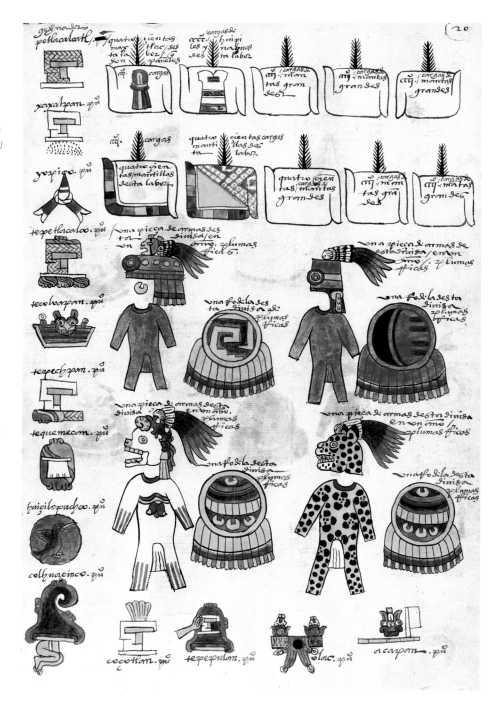

fall loosely over the body. Like the military uniforms themselves the *tilmatli* was ornamented in such a way that soldiers could be recognized for their accomplishments throughout the city: for example, a commoner who had captured one of the enemy was awarded a *tilmatli* ornamented with flowers, two captives earned the right to wear a *tilmatli* dyed orange with a striped border. Consequently, the higher he advanced in rank,

Aztec banners and flags

The large banners secured to the shoulders and backs of high-ranking soldiers and officers were essential to coordinating troop movements. They had to be lightweight so were created by artisans from cloth-covered wicker sewn with hundreds of feathers. According to *Codex Mendoza*, the *quaxolotl* banner (1) was umbrella-like in shape and was produced in yellow, blue, and green. The top was ornamented with the head of a dog called Xolotl whose ears had been ripped off according to a legend. The *tlecocomoctli* banner (2) was supposed to represent a headdress ignited by fire. This example appears in Sahagún's *Primeros Memoriales*. The banner worn by the *huiznahuatl* captain whose name meant "thorn speech" is a variation of the most

basic signal flag or *pamitl* (3). The *chimallaviztli* or "shield insignia" featured the face of a grinning demon (4). The *papalotl* insignia (5) was meant to represent a butterfly. The *caquatonatiuh* meant literally the black and yellow troupial feather sun insignia (6). The strategic significance of such banners was illustrated at Otumba. The army of over 10,000 Aztecs was coordinated by a signal unit under the command of the *Cihuacoatl* (7). Cortés boldly charged through the Aztec army and cut down the *Cihuacoatl*. The effect was devastating. Not only were the Aztec troops demoralized, but they appear to have been unable to coordinate any more effective movement than to withdraw in total confusion. (Adam Hook © Osprey Publishing Ltd)

the more elaborate a *tilmatli* he was entitled to wear. The richest were woven, dyed, hand painted, and embroidered with so much attention to detail that Europeans compared them to the finest garments of silk.

A speech attributed to Tlacaelel (cited by Durán in *The History of the Indies of New Spain*, p.234) illustrates the importance of the various clothing and weaponry worn by different ranks of warriors:

> I wish to give more courage to those of strong heart and embolden those who are weak. Know now that the Emperor has willed that the golden garlands, the featherwork, labrets, earrings, armbands, weapons, shields, insignia, rich cloaks, and breechcloths are not to be purchased in the market by brave men. Our sovereign delivers them personally as payment for memorable deeds. Upon returning from the war each of you will receive rewards according to his merits so that you can display proof of your worth to your families and your gods. If any of you should think to later "borrow" such glory, remember that the only reward that awaits you is execution. So fight on, men, and earn your wealth and reputation here at this military marketplace!

The comparison to a market place was more than metaphorical. In ancient societies, the production and consumption of luxury goods in cotton and feathers was restricted to the elite. Commoners were even forbidden to wear jewelry. Royal women were the principal craft producers and so the kings sought to marry many wives not only because they could forge new alliances but because they could enrich themselves by exchanging their artistic creations through dowry, bridewealth, and other gift-giving networks. Considering that a king might marry as many as 20 times, each palace could produce luxury goods to be measured in tonnage. By AD 1200, royal palaces throughout the central and southern highlands began to engage in fiercely competitive reciprocity systems in order to enhance their position in alliance networks. Many would be quick to perceive that the greater a royal house's ability to acquire exotic materials and to craft them into exquisite jewels, textiles, and featherwork, the better marriages it could negotiate. The better marriages it could negotiate, the higher the rank a royal house could achieve within a confederacy and in turn the better access it would have to more exotic materials, merchants, and crafts people. In short, royal marriages promoted syndicates.

The Aztec strategy through military conquest was to subvert the luxury economies of foreign states by forcing them to produce goods for their own unique system of gift exchange, rewards for military valor that made the soldiers of the imperial armies dependent upon the emperor himself for promotion in Aztec society. The outlandish uniforms seen on the battlefield therefore served as graphic proof of the kind of crushing tribute demands the Aztec empire could inflict as well. Surviving records tell us that no

A steward removes uniforms and weapons from a palace armory and displays them before Motecuhzoma II. (Illustration by John Pohl from the *Florentine Codex*)

fewer than 50,000 cloaks a month were sent by the conquered provinces to Tenochtitlán. The prospect of being forced to subvert their artistic skills to the production of military uniforms that were then redistributed to an ever more glory-hungry army of princes and commoners alike must have been a frightening proposition if not an outright insult to those who would challenge the empire.

Campaign and supply

Although many scholars question the size of Aztec armies described in Spanish colonial historical accounts, the fact was that such large armies were indeed feasible if for no other reason than the fact that the Aztecs could amass food and resources unmatched by any other civilization in the New World. We assume that the inequalities between rulers and ruled, a condition of all early civilizations, first developed with the consolidation of social power by ancient tribal "big men": these dominated society by coordinating agricultural labor and supervising the storage and redistribution of crop surpluses, that ensured group survival against drought. A plant ancestor of maize called *teosinte* may have first been nurtured in the wild by prehistoric shamans as "medicine" in the treatment of disease as early as 5000 BC. Eventually human selection encouraged the plant to evolve into a supplementary feasting food employed by individuals seeking to enhance their social status as paramount chiefs. Grains of incipient maize, for example, were too small to constitute a staple. Instead it was probably consumed as *atole*, an intoxicating brew that continues to be used as a celebratory drink throughout rural Mexico today. Once domesticated foods had been established as staples, however, they became available to any Pre-Columbian population interested in shifting from hunting

Carved stone head of an Eagle warrior. Such uniforms were rare and apparently they were reserved for a special order of nobles. (Museo Nacional de Antropologia, Mexico)

and foraging to agriculture and sedentary life. Pre-Columbian agriculture allowed societies to increase their population, but this in turn created a demand for more intensive cultivation. The Aztecs met the challenge by developing a wide variety of agricultural techniques, from constructing terraces on mountain sides to digging hundreds of miles of canals and even creating artificial wetlands. Maize was the equivalent to wheat in Europe or rice in Asia. What made the Mesoamerican diet so spectacularly rich in protein, however, was the steady diet of maize together with beans and squash, nearly precluding the need for meat.

The only domesticated animals the Aztecs relied on were the dog and the turkey. Once the fields had been planted, the crops naturally lured deer and peccary (wild pigs) out of the wilderness so that hunters could kill the animals on the spot or capture them and keep them at home by tethering. In some areas people even kept deer and milked them like domestic animals. Women became the household scientists responsible for raising animals around the home and breeding and nurturing plants in nearby gardens. Men spent most of their time laboring in the fields. Nowhere in the world was so much energy invested in domesticating plants and we owe a debt of gratitude to the ancient

Aztecs for creating what would eventually become the staples of our own dinner tables: corn, beans, squash, tomatoes, and a host of other foods.

The Aztec army depended on two sources of supply, the *calpulli* itself and stores assembled by tributary kingdoms at designated points along the route of march. Much of the food that an individual warrior ate on campaign would have been prepared by his own family or was contributed in tax by the market place vendors. This was to ensure that the army caused as little impact on the economies of allied nations as possible. Any

An Aztec invasion column divides, AD 1450

Following the defeat of an Eastern Nahua city-state, Nezahualcoyotl explains to a Mexica *Tlacochcalcatl* the need for dividing troops into two columns of march. The strategy was intended to conserve local agricultural resources by reducing the consumptive impact of armies that could range upwards of 50,000 men. Nezahualcoyotl, whose name meant "Fasting Coyote," was forced into exile as a youth after the assassination of his father Ixtlilxochitl by the hated Tepanec despot Tezozomoc. He later succeeded in formulating an alliance with the Mexica under Itzcoatl and together the two *tlatoque* destroyed the Tepanec capital of Azcapotzalco. The uniform of the *Tlacochcalcatl* is based on a plate from *Codex Mendoza*.

Nezahualcoyotl's outfit comes from an illustration appearing in *Codex Ixtlilxochitl*. He wears an *ehuatl* or tunic ornamented with rare tropical bird feathers. Coyote ears affixed to his wooden helmet and tipped with the paper banners of a penitent symbolize his name. The small *huehuetl* drum slung over his back was used to personally issue battlefield commands. High lords and others who could afford them wore greaves of metal. Soldiers on the march wore relatively simple clothing. Ranking warriors proudly displayed the capes given to them by the emperor's own hand. The young men assigned to them for training were responsible for packing basic supplies and carrying extra armaments. (Adam Hook © Osprey Publishing Ltd)

serious devastation by an army to crops or the men and women who grew them was to be avoided under all circumstances. All non-military men were expected to put in their share of labor in the *calpulli*'s communal fields. Once the harvest was reaped in October, the maize was husked, dried, and ground in the family compound with *manos* and *metates* of stone. The pulverized meal was then moistened with water, shaped in six-inch (15cm) round flat cakes, and toasted on a hot, flat ceramic disk. With the onset of the war season in November, the wife, mother and sisters of an Aztec warrior shared responsibilities in preparing a host of tortillas, beans, chili peppers and other seasonings as well as jerky of dried venison, peccary, and turkey, to be packed up and carried by the *telpochcalli* boy who was serving the warrior during the coming campaign. Then the warrior's family withdrew to spend four days fasting and praying to the gods for his safety. Later his father would make daily penitential offerings by drawing blood with thorns from his tongue, ears, arms, and legs to ensure that the gods brought his son home safely the following spring.

During the first long-distance campaigns, the Triple Alliance had to rely on porters called *tlamemehque* to transport the bulk of the provisions and equipment. No fewer than 100,000 had accompanied the troops that attacked Coixtlahuaca in 1458 with each carrying as much as 50lb in materiel. Later, as foreign kingdoms throughout southern and eastern Mexico were subjugated, the empire required that they maintain permanent stores to be used by the army when traveling through their territory. Consequently by 1500, the Aztecs would have had little trouble maintaining armies in the hundreds of thousands in the field for years at a time if need be. The Mexica army was mobilized on the basis of units of 8,000 men called *xiquipilli* drawn from each of the 20 *calpulli* of Tenochtitlán. After each *xiquipilli* had been mobilized, the *huey tlatoani* and his advisors had to determine how to most effectively move it out of the city. The solution was to space departure times over a period of several days so that the movement of the army would have the least impact on the ordinary business of the city. Once the army was outside, it probably averaged anywhere between 10 and 20 miles (16–32km) a day depending upon the urgency of a situation or the need to make a surprise assault. The sheer numbers of men involved in the march on Tututepec would have necessitated the need to designate different departure days for each *xiquipilli*. Considering that the Tenochtitlán army was then joined by an army of allies in equal numbers, no fewer than four different routes would have had to be taken, probably explaining the widely divergent pattern of battles recorded throughout southern Mexico during the course of the campaign. The need to divide large invasion armies suggests that the Aztecs were relying on something resembling the "Corps d'Armée" employed in 18th- and 19th-century Europe in which armies were divided into self-sufficient bodies of troops that moved *en masse* along separate but parallel routes toward a pre-determined destination. The tactical assumption was that each corps would be large enough to pin down any opposing army that got in its way until it could be joined by another. When an enemy had been fully engaged, the corps commander would send runners out to alert the rest

tequiua.

cabtiuo.

cabtiuo.

el mismo alfaqui de atras conto porque ver cabtiuo en la guerra a vnico de sus enemigos por señal de su valentia de le hizo de m. la denisa de cremas Otiene puesta

El mismo alfaqui de atras conto porque ver cabtiual en la guerra de sus enemigos y por señal de su esfuerço y valentia de le hizo de m. la denisa de armas Otiene puestas

cabtiuo.

cabtiuo.

cabtiuo.

quauhnochtli. tecutli

tlilancalqui. tecutli

atenpanecatl. tecutli

ezguaguacatl. tecutlis

Y estos quatro destas hazes eran nombres y executores delos de mex mandaban y determinaban

tlacochcalcatl.

tezcacoacatl.

ticocyahuacatl.

tocuiltecatl.

Y estos quatro desta hazera eran hombres valientes en las guerras y capitanes de los exercitos mexicanos y personas q exercian cargos de generales delos exercitos

Merchants provided the Aztec emperor and his war council with detailed paintings for military logistics. Here a map is presented to two *tetecuhtin* or high-ranking lords describing how the defenses of a city, appearing in the upper right-hand corner, can best be penetrated. (Illustration by John Pohl from the *Florentine Codex*)

of the army who then endeavored to arrive at the scene of battle within hours and attack the enemy's exposed flanks or rear. Since all Aztec armies were composed of "light infantry," any corps could move fast when the situation demanded, making this strategy particularly effective in even the most rugged terrain.

The coordination of such massive troop movements would have depended on a body of well-trained officers. How the chain of command actually functioned remains unknown, however. The *huey tlatoani* was the commander-in-chief and often took a personal role in field combat, especially during the early days of the empire. Second in command was the *Cihuacoatl* or Snake Woman, a position of paramount importance in the priesthood that was first attained by the first Motecuhzoma's younger half-brother Tlacaelel and was subsequently passed on to his son and grandson. The *Cihuacoatl* was responsible for governing Tenochtitlán in the absence of the emperor, but could also act as commander-in-chief on the battlefield as well. Normally the supreme council of four commanders was directly responsible for the army during campaign. Each fulfilled a different role in terms of organizing supply lines, planning the routes of march, devising battlefield strategy, and directing the actual attack. There were officer ranks equivalent to those of major, colonel, captain and so forth that carried out the plans of the supreme council. The highest rank a commoner could hope to attain was that of a *cuauhpilli*, something like a commander with a knighthood, but all the respect given a high-born lord.

Once supply lines from Tenochtitlán itself were overextended, the army had to rely on stores contributed by tributary city-states along the designated route of march. The Aztec empire was unique in that it did not attempt to secure vast amounts of territory but rather was more concerned with controlling strategic locations along primary routes of commercial exchange. Foreign noblemen placed in high office by the Aztecs became the most powerful in their realms but they were forever indebted to the empire to retain their thrones at tremendous expense to their people. For this reason the Aztecs eventually found it necessary to assign tax collectors to various kingdoms who were supported by permanent garrisons of Aztec troops. Following the conquest of Coixtlahuaca, the empire had devised a number of ingenious strategies for dividing up the confederacies of Eastern Nahua, Mixtec, and Zapotec city-states. Initial tactics were ruthless. Under Motecuhzoma I, defeated populations were either sold into slavery or brutally executed before the Great Temple of Tenochtitlán. The loss of valued labor was then replaced by Aztec populations who instituted new governments modeled on local prototypes. This was especially true of Huaxyacac (Oaxaca City) which even appointed its own king. In other cases, the Aztecs sought to maintain local political systems but subverted them by exploiting factional differences within royal families. We tend to think of ancient Mexican kingdoms as stable entities ruled over by omnipotent warlords who claimed divine rights to their thrones and married many times, not only to expand their alliance networks but also to increase their wealth. This practice, however, produced offspring who, more frequently than not, disputed titles of inheritance and became embroiled in wars of succession that dissipated national cohesion. The Aztecs became masters at spotting weaknesses in foreign kingdoms and selecting their own candidates to support as claimants. Pictographic documents from Coixtlahuaca, for example, indicate that, following Atonal's death, an heir was appointed from a rival dynasty while one of Atonal's wives was appointed tax collector. In other cases, those desperate enough to "bargain with the devil" might actually invite the Aztec army into their territory in order to settle a dispute. On other occasions the disruption of political institutions could be helped along through more devious methods. Among the Eastern Nahua, Mixtecs, Zapotecs and their allies, royal marriages were often planned generations in advance. Once the Aztecs had conquered any single member of a confederation, the *huey tlatoani* or a ranking noble might demand a marriage with a local woman of royal blood. Such acts not only bound the Aztec royal line to that of the defeated but also disrupted predetermined marriage alliance patterns. No matter which strategy was employed the goal was to continually expand a network of foreign kings who could best support any Aztec army that needed to move through their territory in the course of a campaign.

Sorcery was a critical element in Aztec warfare. It might appear to be little more than hocus pocus with magicians performing rituals and making burnt offerings before the onset of battle to invoke the gods to punish the enemy. The darker reality of their craft lay with use of plants like oleander from which they generated a poisonous smoke that caused severe nausea, vomiting, and even death when sent out on the wind. Contaminating food and water with disease was a slower but no less effective method for defeating an entrenched enemy who otherwise appeared impervious to siege. Palace curers even became killers when assassination was deemed necessary to resolve conflicts among royal family members.

Field combat

The Aztecs were not usually concerned with positional war, or war for the possession of a defined battlefield area unless it served some particular purpose. Their goal was to maneuver the enemy into situations of entrapment and this demanded perfect coordination and timing. The first order of business was to raise a system of battlefield signals. This was achieved by establishing a command post on an adjacent hill with a direct sight line to the army. Signals were sent by relay. Runners were spaced out at 2½-mile (4km) intervals. Smoke was effective for communicating at longer distances between the *xiquipilli*, as were "heliographs" made from polished iron pyrite mirrors. When engaging in actual combat, however, commanders relied on the enormous ornamental standards together with conch shell horns and drums. Lifting and waving was the principal means of getting the attention of the specific unit signified by a particular banner. Variance in the cadence of the musical instruments directed the unit into action. Field officers watched and listened for the messages. Once the battleline had extended itself, they then walked up and down the rear using whistles to get their men's attention and barked out orders of attack or withdrawal depending on the progress of combat. Battles were generally opened with a good round of insults from both sides. For this reason the *cuahchique* were fond of wearing their hair in tufts, much like professional clowns, and even acted out skits mimicking the enemy's

Musicians such as these were stationed with a signal banner corps to relay messages across the battlefield. A *teponaztil*, a *huehuetl*, and a conch shell trumpet are featured. (*Florentine Codex*, Bk 8 Ch. 17, American Museum of Natural History)

weaknesses in their efforts to get him to break ranks. The most obscene gestures of all imaginable kinds were especially popular and frequently involved exposing the buttocks and genitals. Even women and children were welcome to join in if the

An Aztec squadron surprises the Huaxtecs, AD 1454

The Aztecs frequently employed a ruse, pretending to retreat in order to draw an enemy into an area especially prepared for ambush. When Motecuhzoma I faced a particularly fearsome army of Huaxtecs during his invasion of northern Veracruz, he ordered 2,000 troops to dig holes and conceal themselves under straw. The regular army then executed a successful feint at their center and began to disengage in retreat. The eager Huaxtecs followed in hot pursuit. Once they had passed into their midst, the secret army then literally rose from the ground and slaughtered the terrified enemy. Such war by deception was war by evasion; it was only executed successfully with careful planning, effective signaling, and perfect unit maneuvering. The

Huaxtecs spoke a language closely related to that of the Maya of Central America but linguists still debate when they actually established themselves on Mexico's Gulf Coast. The Aztecs described them as frightening in their appearance with heads purposefully elongated or flattened having had their skulls bound as infants. Some had their teeth filed to points and many sported intricate tattoos. Many shunned the *maxtlatl* or breech clout, and they were accused of being lascivious drunkards. According to one legend Tezcatlipoca seduced the daughter of the King of Tollan by posing as a Huaxtec chili seller, the "chili" in mind referring to the Huaxtec's member. (Adam Hook © Osprey Publishing Ltd)

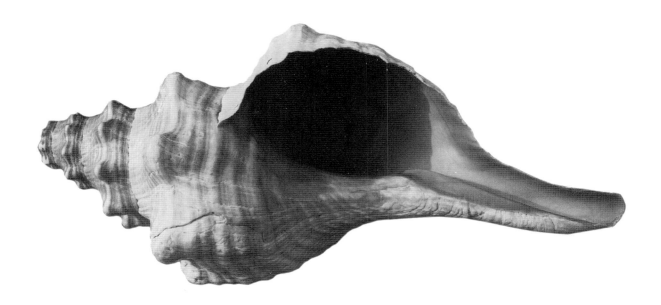

A popular instrument among many ancient civilizations, the conch was capable of issuing a modulated, bellowing sound that could be heard for miles. (John Pohl)

opportunity presented itself. Threats of extreme torture and cannibalism were considered especially inflammatory.

Hostilities generally opened with a mutual barrage of arrows, darts, and sling bullets at 50 yards in an effort to disrupt formations. The Aztecs employed bowmen and slingers from conquered provinces who could be deployed as mobile units either at the front of the line to instigate combat after which they retired to the rear, or directed to the flanks to lay down harassing fire. Frontline veterans were reliant on their superior armor and heavy, broad shields to withstand the rain of enemy projectiles; but sufficient injuries were soon inflicted among the youngest and most lightly armed troops, so that a charge would soon become a necessity. Aztec war was a running war. The vanguard depended on sheer inertia to try to smash through the enemy line and downhill attacks were considered optimal. The subsequent impact must have been horrific. Once troops on both sides had recovered, however, combatants would disperse widely into one-on-one engagements so that they could swing their deadly weapons unhindered. Slashing and parrying with the *macuahuitl* and shield demanded a tremendous expenditure of energy and so men were circulated every 15 minutes in order to keep the center strong. Officers kept a sharp eye out for any weaknesses in the enemy's formation and directed "flying" reserves of veterans to fill gaps among their own men as needed. Ultimately, the Aztecs preferred to surround their enemies and entrap them by double envelopment. This tactic could be dangerous, as it necessitated extending the flanks at the expense of maintaining a strong center. The Aztecs offset the problem by ensuring that they always fought with superior numbers. A surrounded and frightened enemy would fight to the death if they thought their lives were at stake. Aztec commanders therefore tried to induce controlled retreats along prescribed routes where panicked troops could be exposed to easy slaughter by reserves concealed in adjacent corn-fields, trenches, fox-holes, and even under piles of loose grass and leaves.

Bringing home the war: Aztec religion and ritual

Human sacrifice was paramount in Mexican religion, and the Mexicans took it to the extreme. Countless people – slaves, captives, human levies of tribute from the provinces, children of the poor – died on the temples each year. Warfare, human sacrifice, and the promotion of agricultural fertility were inextricably linked in religious ideology. Blood was shed to postpone the inevitable death of the fifth sun, the sun of the Mexicans. They believed it would be the last sun, and when it died, the world would rise no more. The people invented war to feed the sun his holy food and thereby perpetuate life on earth. The Mexicans didn't use the term human sacrifice nor did they consider their ritual activities in any way connected to such a practice as it was later cast on them by Europeans. For them it was *nextlaualli* – sacred debt payment to the gods. Gods had given their own blood to create this sun, and without blood, it would die. The blood of the gods themselves had to be replenished, or they, too, would die. In short, their religion offered no hope, only doom.

The Aztecs had myths which linked the defense of Tenochtitlán to the religious ideology, particularly the myth of the patriarch Huitzilopochtli. A long time ago there lived a woman named Coatlicue, Lady Serpent Skirt, together with her 400 sons. The woman always performed her penance dutifully sweeping on Snake Mountain near the ancient Toltec city of Tollan. One day as she was attending to her chores she gathered up a ball of feathers, placed them at her waist, and miraculously conceived another child. When her 400 sons saw that their mother was pregnant they were enraged. Their sister Coyolxauhqui arrived and addressed them all saying:

> My elder brothers, she has dishonored us, we can only kill our mother, the wicked one who is now with child.

At first Coatlicue was terrified at what her children were plotting. Then just as suddenly a young warrior sprang forth from her womb fully armed. Huitzilopochtli stood atop Coatepec ready to defend his mother against the coming onslaught. Coyolxauhqui dashed to the top of the hill but Huitzilopochtli struck her down with a mighty blow from his spear thrower and lopped off her head. Her body twisted and turned as it fell to the ground at the foot of the mountain. Huitzilopochtli cast down the 400 brothers in equal measure, slew them, and took their raiment as warriors for himself in commemoration of his conquest.

It was the sworn duty of each and every Aztec soldier to carry on the legacy of the great patriarch Huitzilopochtli, the Hummingbird of the South, to be ever vigilant, ever prepared to protect his family, his *calpulli*, and his city from those who would destroy all that his ancestors had worked so hard to accomplish.

Every captive who walked up the steps to the temple represented the hated siblings who in their jealousy would have slain Huitzilopochtli. Each would reenact the role of the cosmic enemy, living proof of the god's omnipotent power manifest in the abilities of his spiritual descendants, his mighty warriors, to repay him for his blessings, indeed the very livelihood that they enjoyed. When a captive reached the top of the stairs, he would be stretched out on his back over a stone and held down by four priests. Then a fifth priest drove a knife into the captive's chest, the trauma of the blow killing him nearly instantaneously. Just as quickly the priest slit the arteries of the heart and lifting the bloody mass into the air pronounced it to be the "precious eagle cactus fruit," the supreme offering to the Sun god Tonatiuh. The heart was then burned in a special vessel carved in the shape of an eagle. The lifeless corpse of the captive was simply tossed back down the staircase.

Among more ancient Mesoamerican societies like the Mayas, Mixtecs, and Zapotecs, war was the province of elite factions, close relatives and kin, who seized each other's lands and property by presenting rival claims of legitimacy through descent from divine

The *Florentine Codex* depicts the execution of war captives whose hearts were torn from their bodies. (*Florentine Codex* Bk 8, Ch. 17, American Museum of Natural History)

Gladiatorial combat at the Great Temple

Tlahuicol was a Tlaxcaltecan captain, sworn enemy of the Aztecs and their hated empire. He was captured and, due to his high rank, forced to participate in the ritual of gladiatorial combat before the Great Temple at Tenochtitlán. Armed only with mock weapons, his wits, and his fists, he succeeded in single-handedly killing no fewer than eight heavily armed jaguar and eagle warriors. He was subsequently offered a command position in the Imperial army. He declined, declaring it to be an insult and voluntarily offered himself in sacrifice to the Aztec war-god Huitzilopochtli whose temple looms in the background. The unusual ritual garb with which Tlahuicol is dressed is the raiment of a war god known as Xipe Totec. Ritual combats were immensely popular. They brought the reality of combat home to a people who had

invested so much in food and materiel, and risked the very lives of their sons. Large circular stones thought to have been employed for gladiatorial combat are displayed in Mexico's National Museum of Anthropology and the Museum of the Great Temple. Both portray images of an Aztec emperor dressed as Huitzilopochtli capturing the gods of enemy city states. By sponsoring festival sculpture of this kind, the *huey tlatoani* clearly sought to combine spectacular showmanship with personal propaganda by reminding the audience of his role as the representative of Tenochtitlán's mightiest warrior. Military success packaged in this way appealed to patriotic and imperialist impulses in the public while providing a potent form of entertainment garnering popular admiration and gratitude. (Adam Hook © Osprey Publishing Ltd)

ancestors. It was not enough to simply kill an enemy in a remote field. Successful usurpers had to display their captives before assembled lineage members, to dispatch their enemies in accordance with their exalted positions as divine rulers, and to demonstrate publicly the institution of a new social order. Heads of state recreated the

Sahagún's *Primeros Memoriales* depicts an Aztec captain wearing an *ehuatl* or tunic of feathers sewn to a cotton backing. Although feathers were certainly employed to ornament the skirt for ritual dress, this reconstruction features heavy leather strips more conducive to battlefield conditions. (Reconstruction by John Pohl)

events of battle through festivals in order to foster public trust. Nowhere did this practice find greater expression than among the Aztecs. Thousands of Aztec people participated in these events, reassuring themselves that their investment in supplying food, making weapons and equipment, and committing the lives of their children would grant them the benefits of conquest that their emperors guaranteed.

Toward the end of the first decade of the 16th century, the appearance of a comet set off a chain of omens that appeared over the ensuing years and foretold the end of the Aztec empire. The comet was followed by a fire that destroyed the Temple of Huitzilopochtli, and the destruction of a second temple by a bolt of lightning, both signs of defeat and conquest. On a calm, still day, the waters of Lake Texcoco rose and flooded the city, destroying many houses. Then, a phantom woman appeared in the night, wailing, "O my beloved sons, now we are at the point of going! My beloved sons, whither shall I take you?" (This particular phantom has passed into modern Mexican folklore as "the llorona," the weeping woman, who is used to frighten children.) Other omens and visions appeared, including one of armed men riding on large animals that appeared to be deer.

Some of these events have rational explanations and were simply natural phenomena: comets appear, lightning strikes, and buildings burn. Geologically, Mexico is extremely unstable, and a distant earthquake easily could have caused the lake to overflow. Yet for all their architecture, organizational ability, and military skill, the Aztecs (like their European counterparts) simply did not understand the natural forces that affected them. Thus, it was easy for their imaginations to make the jump from reality to fantasy, just as it was easy for the New England Puritans, more than a century later, to regard natural occurrences as signs of God's pleasure or wrath.

As high priest of a fatalistic religion, Motecuhzoma could only surmise that the sun of the Aztecs was nearing its end. In 1519, when couriers from the east coast brought word of newcomers wrapped in clothing of silver metal and mounted on strange beasts, he appears to have expected it. He was aware of the Spanish presence in the Gulf of Mexico and Central America; the Mexican trade network was extensive, and so was its intelligence capabilities. In fact, the arrival of Europeans in the region had already worked its way into the latest round of religion and prophecy.

Before long, word reached Motecuhzoma that first the Totonacs and then the Tlaxcalteca had declared the leader of this bizarre enemy to be nothing less than the great god Quetzalcoatl, now returned to reclaim his kingdom from his mortal enemies, Tezcatlipoca and Huitzilopochtli. There were always prophecies of doom but this one was to be considered a serious threat. The Eastern Nahuas, Mixtecs, and Zapotecs all revered the Plumed Serpent as their patron god. Their kings and queens were even accustomed to calling themselves the "Children of Quetzalcoatl." The prophecy of his return in the Aztec year One Reed would be taken as nothing less than a call to abandon their petty disputes and to rise up together as independent nations to overthrow the yoke of Aztec imperialism forever.

PART THREE

THE SPANISH INVASION OF MEXICO

OUTBREAK

In 1519, Diego Velásquez drafted a contract listing Cortés's responsibilities for a forthcoming expedition to Mexico. This being an expedition above all to serve God, blasphemy, gambling, and sleeping with women were, of course, expressly prohibited. The fleet was to keep together and travel west along the coast following the route of Grijalva. All Indian populations that they encountered were to be informed of the power of the king of Spain and his demand that they place themselves under his protective authority. A treasurer and inspector were to be appointed to collect and record all objects of precious metals and stones. Landings were only permitted for the purpose of gathering wood, food, and water. Cortés was to discover the nature of gold sources especially in the Totonac area of Veracruz and to determine the truth of reports of Amazons and half-human creatures. To these instructions Cortés had been careful to add an escape clause, which gave him powers to carry out actions not detailed in the contract, and to act as a legal authority.

The arrangement between Velásquez and Cortés called for the governor to provide two or three ships, with Cortés funding the balance of the expedition. Cortés moved rapidly, assembling his own group of captains, including Pedro de Alvarado, who would serve more or less as his right-hand man throughout the Conquest. Alvarado was ruthless and rash, often prone to acting without considering the consequences, but he would be loyal to Cortés until the end. Others, likewise, could be counted on to support Cortés in any showdown, among them Cristóbal de Olíd and Gonzalo Sandoval. As for the men, the lure of shares in any profit was enough to draw ample recruits from the rootless young adventurers in Cuba, among them a Castilian of good family and little means named Bernal Díaz del Castillo, whose later account would become one of the greatest sources of information on the Conquest.

OPPOSITE
Romantic rendering of the Spaniards fleeing Tenochtitlán. (Topfoto)

ABOVE
Gunners from the *Codex Monacensis 222.* (John Pohl)

A veteran of Columbus's second expedition in 1493, Don Diego Velásquez (1464–1524) arrived in Cuba in 1511 to become the colony's first governor. Although he commissioned Cortés to explore the Mexican hinterland, he distrusted him, regarding him as a rival for the riches waiting to be exploited in the new colonies. (Museo Nacional de Antropología, Mexico)

While he awaited the governor's final permission, Cortés had succeeded in recruiting 300 men by advertising the expedition via Santiago's town crier. Within two weeks of his appointment he had assembled sufficient arms, artillery, and munitions on credit. Weavers were even commissioned to fabricate cotton Indian-style jackets of quilted armor. Cortés purchased a *caravel* and a *brigantine* which, with Alvarado's ship, brought the total to three. Four more would join him shortly.

Watching the preparations in Santiago de Cuba, Velásquez became alarmed at their speed and thoroughness, and feared (with good reason as it turned out) that Cortés might have his own agenda. For his part, Cortés began to suspect that the governor would grab the wealth and glory of a successful expedition, and redoubled his efforts to retain control. Finally, Velásquez forced the issue, and sent orders removing Cortés from command and detaining the expedition. But Cortés had second-guessed him and, on November 18, 1518, ordered the expedition to sail from Santiago.

Nevertheless, the expedition was still short of food, men, and supplies. Cortés stopped at Pilón on Cape Cruz and received 1,000 rations of cassava bread from a friend with a plantation in the area. He also directed one of his ships to sail to Jamaica to acquire 800 sides of bacon in addition to 2,000 more rations of bread. Next, the army landed further west at Trinidad where the local magistrate had been instructed to detain Cortés and remove him as commander. Cortés met with his officers and by invoking autonomous powers in his contract, persuaded them to allow him to retain command. One of his lieutenants, Ordás, proved his loyalty by immediately seizing a passing ship that was loaded with supplies for the colony of Darien in Panama, a bold act that could be taken for piracy. By now 200 more soldiers had joined the expedition; many had just returned with Grijalva and recognized the potential of this operation proposed by a more aggressive commander.

Horses were obtained from the magistrate of Trinidad who ignored Velásquez's orders to arrest Cortés, doubtless on a promise of a share in profits. Descendants of those originally brought from Spain by Columbus, these horses could cost as much as 3,000 pesos each. They were short-legged, but sturdy enough to carry a man in armor on a heavy Moorish saddle. Dogs were also recruited. Wolf hounds and mastiffs had proved effective in battle since medieval times, and packs were particularly useful in combat

The landing of the Spaniards from the *Florentine Codex*, plate I. (American Museum of Natural History)

ESTE ESTANDARTE FUE EL QUE TRAJO Dⁿ FER-NAN-DO COR-TES EN LA CONQUIS-TA DE MEXICO

The banner of the Conquest. Most of the Conquistadores believed their survival was entirely due to the protection of Christ and the saints, and this ensured that their religious observances were regular and fervent. (Topfoto)

against indigenous light infantry. Finally, and perhaps most important to the diplomatic success of the expedition, were large quantities of glass beads, bells, mirrors, needles, and pins, as well as iron knives, scissors, tongs, hammers, and axes – objects that had become commonplace in European societies since Roman times but were unheard of in Mesoamerica. Gift-giving was the primary form of aristocratic social exchange among the civilizations of Mexico. Glass was unknown and so simple beads became priceless in an economy where they had never previously existed; furthermore their possession became the mark of those who had access to new trading partners and exotic forms of commerce in general. Although metallurgy had been adopted from South America by AD 900, it was practiced by royal craft specialists for the production of gold, silver, copper jewelry and other prized commodities. The iron objects that the Spaniards introduced were regarded with much the same sense of exotic value and fascination.

By February 1519, enough supplies had been loaded to last 500 men the few weeks it would take to reconnoiter the coastline from Yucatán to Veracruz, after which the expedition expected to survive on local resources through trade or seizure. Veterans of the previous expeditions recommended loading as many barrels of water as possible, as supplies were frequently unpredictable and could be defended by hostile communities. Cortés needed to ensure that he could feed and water his men on his own terms and not become subject to the desperate acts of starvation and thirst that had endangered the Córdoba and Grijalva expeditions.

Altogether, the fleet that left San Cristóbal on February 10, 1519 consisted of 11 vessels, four of them decked ships, and the rest open brigantines. There were 530 Europeans, several hundred West Indian natives and Africans, as well as about eight European women. Livestock included horses, and a large number of war dogs.

Arms included crossbows, arquebuses, and artillery, as well as flags. Cortés's own standard was blue and white with a red cross in the center. Emblazoned on it was a motto reminiscent of Constantine the Great: *"Amici, sequamor crucem, et si nos fidem habemus, vere in hoc signo vicemus"* ("Friends, let us follow the cross, and if we have faith, truly by this sign we shall conquer"). Cortés dedicated the expedition itself to St. Peter, who he believed took a special interest in his safety.

Route of Cortés from Cuba to Mexico.

Cortés and Doña Marina

When Cortés arrived off the coast of Veracruz, he received an Aztec ambassador who was directed by Motecuhzoma to honor him as Quetzalcoatl, the Plumed Serpent. The year 1519, it seems, was the equivalent of the Aztec year One Reed, a date specifically associated with the legend of the Toltec man-god. Cortés stands at the center of the deck wearing the turquoise inlaid mask, the *quetzal* plume headdress of the god, and a *xicolli* or fringed jacket worn by priests. On Cortés's right stands Pedro de Alvarado who was himself treated as a divinity, the sun god Tonatiuh, because of his red hair. Why Cortés, a devout Catholic, allowed himself to be venerated as the returning pagan god Quetzalcoatl is a mystery. Having studied classical history at the University of Salamanca he may have had some elementary knowledge of the relationship of hero cults to the alliances of Greek city-states, and he may have possibly compared himself to the Renaissance princes who had themselves immortalized in marble or paint as Classical Roman gods.

In any case, Cortés's friars would have told him that Quetzalcoatl was no less than the Hercules of the New World. Conquistadores soon learned that there were tremendous political advantages in accommodating such rituals. Stories of returning gods were just one means by which factions in Indian societies could assert their agendas and legitimize their demands for changes in social and political order. Pizarro was also invoked as the fulfillment of a prophecy of a returning Inca hero named Viracocha. In a remarkable twist on the theme, Spaniards on a later expedition to the Petén jungle of Guatemala were surprised to learn from one Maya lord that the year prophesied for their invasion had not yet arrived and that they should return at a later date or face death. When they did as he advised, they found themselves being used as pawns in a power struggle between the lord and his rivals, all of whom were invoking the prophecies of the sacred calendar to promote themselves into high office.

Next to Cortés stands the mysterious Indian girl known to history as Doña Marina. Although her existence and role are well documented, details of her life are sparse, conflicting, and shrouded in legend. The Mexican view of her is schizophrenic. On the one hand, she is *La Malinche* who betrayed her people. Yet as the mother of Cortés's son Martín, the first recorded *mestizo* or mixed-blood that makes up the bulk of the modern Mexican population, she is the mother of the nation. This ambiguity, no doubt, stems to a large degree from her importance. In assuming her decisive position, willingly or otherwise, she went against the established norm of female nonentity expected in both Spanish and Aztec society, a status that combined and carried over into the traditional Mexican view of women.

Her origins are shrouded in contradiction. At the time she was acquired by the Spanish she was about 17. It is almost certain her name was Malinalli, Hispanicized to Marina. Bernal Díaz invariably appended "doña" as a title of respect, possibly for her position as interpreter, or possibly for her position as Cortés's mistress, or both. He called her a "great chieftainess and daughter of chieftains and mistress over vassals, and one could see this by her carriage."

Most of the information concerning Doña Marina comes from Bernal Díaz, who was the only contemporary writer to give a woman a significant role in the great events of the age. Others mention her, but in Díaz's *True History*, she holds an honored position almost equal to Cortés himself. Díaz, who was not writing with the hope of any serious personal gain, appears to have recognized, more than the others that without her, there would have been no Conquest. López de Gómara downplayed Doña Marina's role as much as Díaz played it up, and of the two, Díaz is the more believable. Her true role was probably somewhere between that of servant-concubine and Conquistadora. It is doubtful that Cortés would have accomplished so much – if indeed anything at all – without her help. As much as a feat of arms, the Conquest of Mexico was a triumph of diplomacy, in recognizing and exploiting the divisions and hatreds between the various Indian states. Doña Marina was essential to the Spaniards' understanding of all the implications of local rivalries. Given the bond that existed between Marina and Cortés during the Conquest, there can be little doubt that Marina's loyalty was based on love and admiration as much as servitude. For his part, Cortés seemed to view women in general as a means of pleasure or policy, but if he was capable of love, his attention toward Marina is some indication. Cortés on campaign, however, was not the same as Cortés projecting his image to the Spanish court and to posterity. Barring the possibility of some mention in his now lost First Letter, Marina appears only twice in his correspondence, once in the Second Letter, in which he refers to her as "my interpreter, who is an Indian woman from Putunchan," and in the Fifth, written more than four years later, where he called her "Marina, who traveled always in my company after she had been given me as a present with twenty other women." Through the pen of López de Gómara, Cortés acknowledged his illegitimate children by Marina and others, nevertheless, the relationship itself is carefully skirted. Whatever Cortés might have felt for Marina, he could not expect to present himself at court as the harbinger of civilization and champion of Christianity while having an intense and history-making affair with an Indian girl. Yet, reading between the lines of his letters, there is no question that he depended on her.

In 1522, Marina gave birth to Martín Cortés, the conqueror's eldest son. Two years later, Cortés married her off to Juan Jaramillo. She also received estates in Tabasco, where she apparently spent most of her time until her death in 1551. The Conquest was the great event of Doña Marina's life; after it, she gradually faded from history. Even so, her essential role in Cortés's success cannot be disputed. (Adam Hook © Osprey Publishing Ltd)

The main plaza at Cempoala, just one example of the superb architecture that amazed the Conquistadores. (© Philip Baird, www.anthroarcheart.org)

The initial landing

In the Yucatán Channel heavy weather scattered the fleet and, according to a prearranged plan, all but one of the ships rendezvoused at Cozumel, off the west coast of the Yucatán Peninsula, an island already well known to Spanish pilots. About one-third of his men had already been there with Grijalva. Here, Cortés was at his best, treating the locals in such a friendly manner that he had little trouble establishing contact. Communication was through the broken Castilian of "Old Melchor," a Maya who had been taken to Cuba on the Córdoba expedition of 1517. Soon, however, they received an unexpected bonus in the person of Jerónimo de Aguilar, an Andalusian cleric who had been shipwrecked on the island in 1511, and who now spoke fluent Chontal Maya. One of two survivors of the wreck, he readily joined the expedition. His companion, Gonzalo Guerrero, however, had married into the local nobility with a high position, and ignored letters inviting him to be repatriated.

The stay in Cozumel gave Cortés time to plan his next move, and to accustom his band of mercenaries and adventurers to working together as a cohesive, disciplined unit. Sailing from Cozumel, the fleet touched at nearby Isla Mujeres, then continued on around the Yucatán Peninsula to Tabasco, in the Gulf of Mexico. On March 22 they entered the waterway now known as the Rio Grijalva, where Cortés, through Aguilar, attempted a parley with natives from the nearby town of Potonchán. The locals, however, were hostile and, the following day, he forced his way ashore. The decisive fight came on Annunciation Day, March 25. Whipped up by Old Melchor, who had escaped and joined them, the Indians fought fiercely, but the landing of the horses and the new experience of a cavalry charge sent them fleeing in panic.

The large numbers of native warriors and their tough resistance convinced Cortés that force would not be enough to subjugate the mainland peoples, as it had been with the islands of the Indies. The key would be diplomacy, to overawe with words, and with display, and to look for and exploit weaknesses and factionalism.

Summoning the chiefs, he told them that if they became vassals of the Spanish Crown, as were the Spaniards themselves, he would protect them. Otherwise, he said the artillery (which he represented as living creatures), would jump up and kill them. That was the signal for one of the gunners to fire his piece. At the same moment, one of the more assertive stallions was allowed to scent a mare that had recently foaled, and he began to paw and buck. The terrified chiefs immediately submitted and the following morning brought gifts of gold, fine cloth, along with 20 women to serve the Spaniards as "wives." Asked where the gold originated, they answered "Culhua," referring to the Valley of Mexico, and "Mexico," referring to the Aztec capital itself.

Cortés and his men now determined to visit Mexico to see for themselves the source of this wealth. The most important gift from the chiefs of Potonchán suddenly became one of the women, a girl in her late teens named Malinalli. Renamed Doña Marina, she spoke both Nahuatl and Chontal, so she could communicate with the Mexicans and with Aguilar, and thus became Cortés's ears and mouthpiece. Years later in his account of the Conquest, Bernal Díaz would write, "Doña Marina in all the wars of New Spain and Tlaxcala and Mexico was a most excellent woman and good interpreter... [and] in this capacity she always accompanied Cortés." Almost as an afterthought, he added she also became Cortés's mistress and bore him a son.

Getting under way again, the fleet sailed for four days, arriving at the island of San Juan de Ulúa, at the entrance to the modern harbor of Veracruz, on Maundy Thursday. Although this was the country of the Totonacs, a people subject to Mexico, the dignitaries

The Temple of the Warriors at Tollan (Tula, Hidalgo), the first Toltec capital. The atlantid figures are thought to represent either the Chichimec hero Camaxtli-Mixcoatl or his son Quetzalcoatl in the guise of the god of the Morning Star. (John Pohl)

who came out in canoes appear to have been Mexican. Inviting them on board his ship for dinner, Cortés told them through Aguilar and Doña Marina that he came as a friend to trade and explore. The following day, he led his men ashore, setting up camp with an altar to celebrate Good Friday Mass. All the while, more dignitaries were arriving, culminating on Easter Sunday with a visit from Tentlil, a sort of governor apparently charged with overseeing Mexican affairs in the province and keeping the Totonacs in line.

Cortés explained his mission, and said he looked forward to meeting Motecuhzoma. Tentlil replied that this was impossible. However, the emperor had sent magnificent gifts of gold, cloth, and featherwork. Cortés responded by giving European goods unfamiliar in the New World, such as glass beads and a finely carved chair. His men demonstrated their horsemanship skills and mastery of artillery before the governor.

Tentlil departed, returning again in a few days with even greater treasures, among them a gigantic, beautifully decorated golden disc representing the sun, and a slightly smaller one representing the moon. Before leaving, he had borrowed a European helmet, and now returned it filled to the top with gold dust. A meeting between Cortés and the emperor, however, was apparently impossible.

Motecuhzoma's reasons for offering these great treasures have been debated for almost five centuries. Was he trying to bribe the Spaniards into leaving? Or was he attempting, as often was done in the Orient, to overawe these foreigners with his wealth and power? Whatever the motive, it only excited the Spanish, and made them more determined to visit the source of such wealth. The problem was that the camp was divided into two factions: the supporters of Diego Velásquez, who wanted to take what had been gained so far and depart for Cuba, and the rank and file, who saw little advantage in supporting the governor but unlimited opportunities in moving ahead.

Cortés's position was simple. He had to conquer or die. If he returned to Cuba, he faced imprisonment or death for sailing in defiance of the governor. To advance on his own would make him a traitor to the Crown – unless he were backed by a legally constituted authority. His brief training in law had prepared him for this day. He resigned the commission given him by Velásquez, thus absolving him of all allegiance to the governor, persuaded the men to form a municipal government, designated Villa Rica de la Vera Cruz ("Rich Town of the True Cross," subsequently moved 40 miles north up the coast, where the Spaniards established the first permanent town, now a ruin), and petitioned the king to recognize it as a colony, with Cortés as captain and chief justice. The treasure accumulated to date was inventoried and loaded aboard ship to accompany Cortés's representatives, Alonso Hernández Puertocarrero and Francisco de Montejo, back to Spain. This, technically, was a pledge of good faith, but in fact was a bribe to the avaricious King Charles.

While camped on the coast, the Spaniards were visited by a delegation from the principal Totonac city of Cempoala, whose primary mission seemed to have been to assess the potential of these strangers as allies against their Mexican overlords. Taking the bulk of his force, Cortés marched inland to the city, which had been wealthy and powerful in its own right, although was now a tributary to Mexico. Here, the Spaniards saw the first examples of the magnificent architecture and large populations they would increasingly encounter as they moved inland. They also saw very real indications of extensive human sacrifice on the blood-soaked temples.

The Totonacs apparently were on the verge of rebellion, and Cortés played this to his advantage. By lucky coincidence, the Mexican tribute gatherers arrived in the Totonac towns. Angry that the Spaniards had been received without permission, they demanded, in addition to the usual tribute, 20 men and women for sacrifice. Cortés convinced the Totonacs to arrest them, saying the Spanish Crown intended to end such abuses. The proud officials were dragged through the streets in halters, and one was flogged. That night, however, they were permitted to escape, and returned to Mexico with the news of a rebellion. Then, in an even more daring move, Cortés ordered the idols thrown down from the Totonac temples, smashed to pieces and burned. When the people tried to stop it, their chiefs and priests were surrounded, and Cortés said they would be killed on the first show of hostility. Having defied their overlords, and with their religion destroyed, the Totonacs were now committed to the Spanish cause beyond any possibility of turning back.

It was then that the Spaniards were invited by a Totonac delegation to meet with their own lord at Cempoala. Learning of their military prowess and believing Cortés to be Quetzalcoatl's representative if not actually the god himself, the Totonacs explained that they had been conquered by the Aztec empire of the Triple Alliance many years before and now suffered oppressive tribute demands. It was the first indication of dissent among Motecuhzoma's vassals and Cortés foresaw considerable advantages in allying himself with the Indians who were traditional enemies of the Aztecs.

The Tlachihualteptl or "Hill of the Idol" at Cholula is arguably the world's largest manmade structure. It was constructed in successive stages between 200 BC and AD 950. While the later Eastern Nahua inhabitants of the city venerated the more ancient pyramid, they were careful to erect a new temple to their own patron god, Quetzalcoatl, about 1000yds to the northeast. It was there that Cortes averted a massacre of his men by initiating one of his own slaughtering thousands of Cholula's citizens. Either the Tlachihualtepetl was never finished or more likely it was meant to represent a manmade mountain complete with flower gardens and springs at the time the Spaniards first visited the city. It is surmounted by a later Colonial church. Staircases and other features have been excavated around the base of the pyramid which measures 960 by 1280ft. Visitors can tour the tunnels into the pyramid that reveal the successive stages of construction. (© Philip Baird, www.anthroarcheart.org)

Cortés meets the Tlaxcalteca
while Doña Marina serves as
interpreter. (*Lienzo de Tlaxcala*,
plate 4; American Museum
of Natural History)

Atlinetzyan.

The Totonacs explained that Quetzalcoatl had founded the Toltec capital of Tula, located about 40 miles north of Mexico City, some 500 years earlier. Here the Toltecs prospered until a rift developed between two opposing factions. When Quetzalcoatl's rivals, Tezcatlipoca and Huitzilopochtli, patron gods of the Aztecs, incited the hero to drunkenness and incest, he was shamed before his followers and left the city to spend the remainder of his life wandering from kingdom to kingdom. By most accounts he established a new cult center at Cholula. Others report that he also traveled through Oaxaca where he even constructed the Zapotec palaces at Mitla. According to the Totonacs, Quetzalcoatl eventually reached their own capital of Cempoala and subsequently either died and was resurrected as the morning star, or boarded a raft of serpents bound for the east, promising to return one day to reclaim his kingdom.

By analyzing the sagas of Mesoamerican cultural heroes like Quetzalcoatl, historians have discovered that their cults played a significant ideological role when independent kingdoms wanted to unite into larger states in Postclassic Mexico. The aim of sharing heroic history was to elevate the ideology of one elite group above the petty disputes of individuals that prevented unity and the mutual benefits of coalition. Since heroes were sanctified by religious ritual, they could be used to incite patriotic sentiments. As a consequence, the spiritual connection to gods, heroes, and ancestors maintained through their cults could be comparable to the claims of nationality and language which contemporary societies use to define a state. The Totonacs, together with the Eastern

Nahua, the Mixtecs, and the Zapotecs, believed themselves to be the "children of Quetzalcoatl." The Totonacs advised that the Spaniards could find sympathetic allies among the Tlaxcalteca, members of an Eastern Nahua confederacy to the west, and provided them with 50 warriors and 200 porters to help move supplies and falconets 100 miles inland.

The Tlaxcalteca

Before heading west, Cortés had to deal with one last piece of unfinished business: a growing rebellion in the Velásquez faction, whose members planned to seize one of the ships and return to Cuba. Moving swiftly, Cortés hanged one of their leaders. Then, having removed everything of any possible use, he scuttled his fleet. Like their leader, the men were now faced with two options: conquer or die.

In mid-June, Cortés left Cempoala for the interior. Passing through the town of Zautla, he heard, for the first time, a detailed description of the city of Tenochtitlán, which filled the men with both excitement and fear. Continuing on up through the Valley of Zautla, they reached a wall built across the western mouth which, they were told, marked the territory of Tlaxcala, a loose confederation of four cities centered around the city of Tlaxcala itself. Locals advised him to stay clear of the country, because the Tlaxcalteca were mortal enemies of the Aztecs; if they knew the Spaniards were going to Tenochtitlán, they would attack. However, heeding the advice of the Totonacs, the Spaniards continued.

According to their own histories, the Tlaxcalteca were among the first Chichimec bands to invade the Basin of Mexico under the leadership of Quetzalcoatl's father, Mixcoatl. After the fall of Tula around the middle of the 12th century, they moved to the east to settle in the modern state of Tlaxcala, confederating themselves with Huexotzinco, Cholula, and a score of smaller kingdoms from Puebla to Oaxaca. Tlaxcaltecan territory was divided into four pie-shaped quarters converging on a central point where government was dominated by the four highest-ranking kingdoms, Tepeticpac, Quiahuiztlan, Ocotelolco, and Tizatlan. Located within a few miles of each other, the rulers of these kingdoms, called *tlatoque*, formed a governing council. The council was led by the *tlatoani* of Tizatlan at the time of the Conquest, but there is evidence of a rotational power structure rooted in a fairly equal distribution of political, religious, and economic functions. Despite the outward appearance of a stable centralized administration, the *tlatoque* governed Tlaxcala in the midst of profound factional tension. The lesser lords, called *tetecuhtin*, frequently competed with each other over inheritance rights, ownership of lands, and access to strategic resources. When news of the Spaniards' arrival reached them, the council was divided over action.

Sending cavalrymen ahead as scouts, Cortés marched into Tlaxcaltecan territory. After about ten miles, the scouts ran into an advance party of about 15 warriors who attacked with spears, killing two horses, and wounding three others, as well as two horsemen. These were soon joined by some 4,000–5,000 warriors. The cavalry moved in and "did them some damage," and as soon as the infantry arrived, the Tlaxcalteca withdrew.

After an uneasy night, fighting began again the next morning. This time, Cortés estimated there were as many as 100,000 warriors, who were held off by artillery, crossbows, musket fire, and cavalry until about an hour before sunset, when the Tlaxcalteca again broke off. The Spaniards retreated to a small hill, fortifying the temple they found on top. At dawn the next day Cortés led a raid that burned several small villages and brought their inhabitants back as prisoners. The Tlaxcalteca responded by assaulting the hill with a force that Cortés estimated at about 149,000 men. Some managed to break the line, and the fighting turned to hand-to-hand combat, Toledo steel ranged against the razor-like stone weapons of the natives. Cortés continued with his dawn raids against the villages. This, together with the Spanish determination to hold the fort at any cost, was a new concept of war, and the Tlaxcalteca were unsettled. Ultimately they sued for peace, explaining that they had attacked on the presumption that Cortés was allied with Tenochtitlán. The Tlaxcaltec lords realized that a long-term alliance with the Spaniards against their common enemy, the Aztecs, would be of more benefit than the satisfaction of a minor victory over a small group of strangers. Cortés was soon to learn that the Tlaxcalteca were not unique in their behavior. Countless times throughout the campaign, Spanish successes would be due as much to such sudden reversals of policy among Indian factions as any other single factor.

Tlaxcala, the Spaniards learned, was bounded on all sides by Tenochtitlán and its allies, and had been engaged in nearly 60 years of continuous warfare with the Aztecs. Indeed Motecuhzoma later told Andrés Tapia (a conquistador who wrote an account of the conquest in 1545) that the only reason he tolerated the country's existence was that it served as a convenient training ground for young warriors in the "flower wars" that brought enemy captives to Tenochtitlán for sacrifice. Economically it was also at the mercy of

The advance to the city of Mexico, 1519.

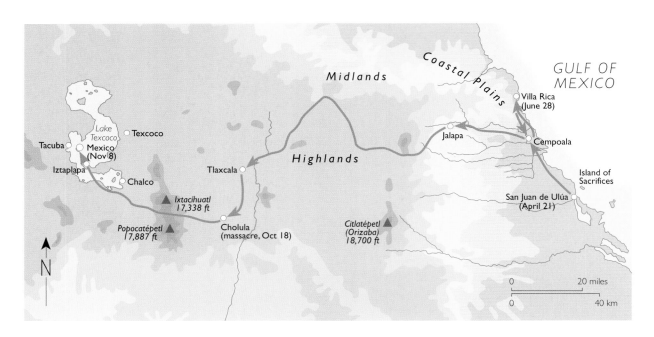

The March on Tenochtitlán

Battle-worn Spanish troops march out of the Valley of Tlaxcala together with their Indian allies. Despite the myth they propagated of their accomplishments, the fall of Tenochtitlán was not accomplished by a few hundred Conquistadores alone, but by a mighty Indian army numbering in the tens of thousands. In June 1519 Cortés marched out of Cempoala at the head of a confederated army of 300 Spaniards and 250 Totonacs who served as both soldiers and a transport corps to carry the food they would need to live on in enemy territory, as well as an artillery of four falconets. When peace was made with the kingdoms of Tlaxcala a second alliance resulted in the commitment of an initial force of 2,000–3,000 more Indian troops. The Cempoalteca and Tlaxcalteca thereby became the nucleus of an allied army that by 1521 was being led by their own heroic conquerors such as Chichimecatecatl of Tlaxcala and Ixtlilxochitl of Texcoco.

The exact numbers of Indian allies are impossible to determine. Cortés reported that he had 50,000 Tlaxcalteca and that ultimately his Indian army numbered 150,000. His biographer, López de Gómara, spoke of 60,000 troops from Texcoco and 200,000 from Tlaxcala, Huexotzinco, Cholula, and a score of other communities. Whatever the exact figures, the indigenous people, men, women and children alike, performed essential logistics work, maintaining the constant supply of weaponry and food, upon which any successful campaign ultimately depends, as well as acting as engineers and sappers constructing roads, bridges, cutting timber for ships and other siege machines, and performing demolition. (Adam Hook © Osprey Publishing Ltd)

Tenochtitlán, because it had few resources and produced little, and was therefore reduced to bartering with its more powerful neighbor. Nevertheless, its warriors were numerous and well organized. Recognizing its potential as an ally, Cortés was careful to emphasize Spanish friendship. Arriving at the city of Tlaxcala, he quartered his men and staked out a sort of military reservation, the limits of which the soldiers were not to cross without permission.

The Tlaxcaltecan alliance proved to be a turning point in the Conquest, for without their massive military power, it is doubtful that a handful of Europeans and Totonac auxiliaries could have defeated Mexico. Tlaxcala remained faithful to the end, and throughout the colonial period was described in Spanish sources as "most loyal." This has earned the modern city and state the disdain of other parts of Mexico, particularly Mexico City, where citizens contend that the country was betrayed by Tlaxcala. Modern Tlaxcalteca, however, are equally touchy about their reasons for siding with Cortés, and are quick to point out all the grievances their country had with Aztec Mexico.

Cholula and the final thrust to Mexico

By Cortés's own account, he spent 20 days in Tlaxcala, when the Mexican emissaries suggested he continue on another 30 or so miles to Cholula, a wealthy, populous trading city allied with Mexico. There, they told him, he could wait and learn whether or not Motecuhzoma would receive him. The Tlaxcalteca were against the idea, claiming it was a trap. Motecuhzoma, they told him, had withdrawn troops from their own borders to strengthen the garrison at Cholula. The main road had been closed, and an alternative path had been constructed, full of pitfalls with sharpened stakes, to neutralize the cavalry. They also pointed out that no delegation from Cholula had come to visit, whereas those of more distant cities had. Cortés, however, remained adamant. He later admitted to the king that part of his determination was to impress the Tlaxcalteca themselves, fearing that any hesitancy might show weakness; he was determined to convince all potential enemies and allies of Spanish invincibility. When the Tlaxcalteca saw Cortés could not be dissuaded, they insisted on sending 100,000 well-armed warriors. Cortés assented, although, as his force neared Cholula, he sent most of the auxiliaries home, keeping only 5,000–6,000 men who were ordered to remain outside of the city, at the request of the Cholulans.

Cholula was a place of pilgrimage. At the time of the Conquest, it had 365 temples, one for each day of the Aztec year, and afterwards churches were said to have been built on each of them. Whether the church-to-temple ratio is entirely accurate is debatable, but modern Cholula must certainly have one of the highest densities of churches in relation to available real estate of any city in Mexico. Then and now, the city was dominated by the Tlachihualteptl, a great pyramid that remains the largest single free-standing structure on earth.

The Cholulans welcomed the expedition with great ceremony, and provided comfortable quarters. Nevertheless, Cortés was suspicious because en route he had verified much of what the Tlaxcalteca had told him. The attitude of the Cholulans, likewise, cooled. Over the next three days, food gradually worsened until, on the third day, it was stopped entirely. Visits by the local dignitaries became less frequent, until they also ceased. Crowds outside the quarters began to jeer and taunt the Spaniards. The ever-vigilant Doña Marina had struck up friendships among the noblewomen, and learned that a massacre was being prepared. This was confirmed by runners from the Tlaxcalteca, who, from their camp, had observed events with growing uneasiness.

The massacre at Cholula, illustrated in a 19th-century history of Mexico. (Collection of Charles M. Robinson)

Cortés summoned the Cholulan leaders and, after hinting that he knew of the plot, said he wanted men as bearers for the trip into Mexico. When the bearers arrived, they were heavily armed and were, in fact, the elite of the warriors. Now, convinced beyond all doubt, Cortés again assembled the Cholulans and deployed his men, telling them that when they heard a musket shot, they were to fall on the Cholulans outside the quarters. When the leaders arrived, they were taken into a courtyard and surrounded. Several were interrogated and confessed to the trap. The signal was given and the slaughter began. Having dispatched those around their quarters, the Spaniards and the Totonac auxiliaries moved out into the city from house to house, hunting down and killing any warrior or potential warrior they could find. Several priests fled to the top of the Tepanapa, but died when the Spaniards set the temple ablaze. Cortés estimated about 3,000 men were killed in the first two hours.

With the city in complete chaos, he now brought in their ancient enemies, the Tlaxcalteca, and allowed them two days of pillage and slaughter. The inhabitants who survived the initial assault fled into the countryside. After several days, they came wandering back into Cholula, begging for mercy. Having made an example of anyone else who might oppose him, Cortés now relented and allowed them to return, promising his protection henceforth.

The Spanish account is different from that of the Aztecs. Sahagún's informants contend that the massacre was instigated by the Tlaxcalteca, and make no mention of a plot by the Cholulans. This is unlikely, however, given Cortés's basic preference for diplomacy, with armed conflict as a last resort. Whatever the case, the news of the massacre shocked

City of Mexico, 1519. Cortés entered the city via the Iztapalapa Causeway on November 18, 1519. The retreat on *La Noche Triste* (June 30–July 1, 1520) was via the Tacuba Causeway. Besides the causeways, the city was intersected by numerous canals that had to be bridged.

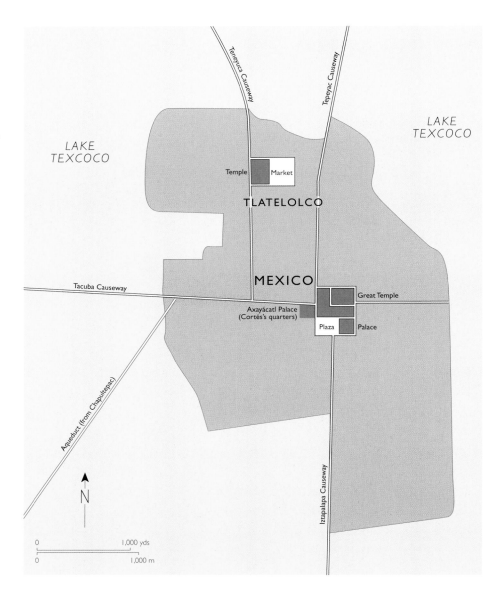

Motecuhzoma and his court; it was the exact opposite of what they had expected. He had intended for the Cholulans to finish the Spaniards, but Cortés anticipated this, and hit first. Once more, the emperor sent emissaries with gifts, this time, however, with a double who would pass himself off as the emperor in a meeting with Cortés.

While the court worried, Cortés prepared for the final thrust to the city of Mexico. The skyline over Cholula is dominated by two giant volcanoes, Popocatépetl and Ixtacíhuatl, each more than 17,000 feet high, rising above the mountains to the west. Popocatépetl, which began a new surge of eruptions in the late 1990s, likewise was active in 1519, and Cortés sent a detachment of soldiers to investigate. At 13,000 feet, they discovered a pass between the mountains and determined from local Indians that a good road led from the pass into the Valley of Mexico. They attempted to climb the mountain, but were forced back short of the summit by the winds, tremors, clouds of ash, and glaciers. Nevertheless, they brought back samples of ice and snow to prove that it existed in a tropical climate.

Departing Cholula, the expedition was met by more ambassadors who offered to lead the way into Mexico by a different road than the one between the mountains. The Tlaxcalteca, however, were suspicious, because the proposed route was through rough country, ideally suited for ambush. Going into camp, Cortés sent a detachment of soldiers with the ambassadors to scout that route, and Diego Ordaz with the Tlaxcalteca to scout beyond the pass. The first group returned with news that the route was impassable. A day later, Ordaz and the Tlaxcalteca returned with an incredible story. The conquistador Alonso de Aguilar later recalled that Ordaz "had seen another new world of large cities and towers, and a sea, and in that sea a very large city, which indeed seemed frightening and awesome." This was the wealthy, powerful Aztec capital of Tenochtitlán, situated on its island in Lake Texcoco.

Descending down onto the plain, they passed through various tributary provinces, whose leaders almost universally complained of Mexican oppression. Ambassadors were sent ahead to the various cities and provinces on the route, and alliances were formed. It became increasingly obvious that these foreigners were seen as liberators, not necessarily benign, but at least the lesser of evils. The Aztec Empire was falling apart, as the years of ruinous tribute and cruelty that had made it the greatest power in North America now worked against it. In Huexotzinco, the leaders warned Cortés that Motecuhzoma would allow them to enter the city, then, having trapped them inside, would massacre them. Similar warnings were given in Amecameca and elsewhere.

En route, they were met by the embassy that included Motecuhzoma's double and which brought gold worth 3,000 pesos. The double (whom Cortés identified as a brother of the emperor), represented himself as Motecuhzoma, but, after consulting with the Tlaxcalteca and Totonacs, Cortés informed him that he knew better. He told the representatives that his own king in Spain had personally dispatched him to visit the capital, meet with Motecuhzoma, and report back, and that he could not disobey. The march continued, while the embassy returned shamefaced, to report to their emperor.

In the years preceding the arrival of the Spaniards, omens in the form of bizarre celestial phenomena were witnessed and interpreted as signs of disaster. (Illustration by John Pohl from the *Florentine Codex*)

Sahagún's Mexican informants told a tale illustrating how devastating the chain of events had become for Mexican morale. In one last desperate attempt to forestall the inevitable, Motecuhzoma sent necromancers and sorcerers out to try to ward off the Spaniards by enchantment. En route, however, they met a traveler who seemed almost berserk with rage. "What does Motecuhzoma pretend to accomplish with your remedies against the Spaniards? He has realized late that they are determined to take his kingdom, whatever he possesses, and even his honor, because of the great tyrannies he has committed against his vassals! He hasn't reigned as a lord, but as a tyrant and a traitor!" The terrified sorcerers listened as the man continued to rant. "Turn around and look at Mexico, and what will happen to her before many days have passed!" Obeying, they turned and saw the city in flames. As they attempted to answer, the stranger disappeared. They now realized that he was Tezcatlipoca, paramount of the gods. Knowing they and their city were doomed, they abandoned their mission. Listening to their report, Motecuhzoma knew his gods had abandoned him, and he was completely alone. He began preparations to receive the Spaniards in the capital itself.

Why Motecuhzoma did not crush the Spaniards with the overwhelming military force he was known to have at his command has always been a source of debate. One theory is that, after Cortés's success in defeating Motecuhzoma's allies and appointing a new king to the throne of Cholula, any further opposition on Motecuhzoma's part might encourage dissident factions within his own domain, particularly around Chalco, a kingdom once allied with Tlaxcala, that had never been absorbed into the empire peacefully. Another theory is that the majority of young men who composed the Aztec imperial forces were also farmers and therefore the principal food producers for the entire city. Armies could therefore only be mobilized during the dry season from November to May when the fields lay fallow. This theory is reinforced by an account of the Yucatán Caste War of 1847. At one point the city of Merida had been surrounded and the governor was considering evacuating the city when suddenly the insurrectionists inexplicably withdrew. Years later it was discovered that the host of Maya farmer-soldiers had seen the first rain clouds of the season approaching and took it as a sign to return to their villages to plant the life-giving maize on which they would have to subsist throughout the following year, even though it meant forfeiting a hard-won victory. Whatever the actual reasons, Motecuhzoma clearly perceived a greater advantage for the moment in inviting the Spaniards into the city of Tenochtitlán. Although it temporarily placed him in a compromising position, it was a logical strategy from the perspective of the political situation at that time.

At Ayotzingo, the Spaniards were met by Motecuhzoma's distant cousin, Cacama, king of Texcoco. He arrived in the splendor befitting a ruler of the Triple Alliance, carried on a litter borne by eight lords of subordinate cities. When he met Cortés, he announced that he had been sent to personally conduct the expedition to the city of Tenochtitlán. Gifts were exchanged, and the prince, his entourage, the Spaniards, and their auxiliaries began the march, crossing the great Cuitláhuac Causeway that separates Lake Chalco

Modern portrait of an Aztec *Huey Tlatoani* or Great Speaker wearing the turquoise crown and royal blue cloak by Scott Gentling and Stuart Gentling. "The Great Motecuhzoma..." wrote Bernal Díaz del Castillo, "...was of good height and well proportioned, slender, not swarthy, but of the natural color of an Indian. He did not wear his hair long, but just so as to cover his ears and his scanty black beard was well shaped and thin. His face was somewhat long, but cheerful, and he had good eyes and showed in his appearance and manner both tenderness and, when necessary, gravity." (Illustration by Scott & Stuart Gentling)

from Lake Xochimilco, and on to Itzapalapa, on the shores of Lake Texcoco itself. Here, the lords of Itzapalapa and Coyoacán met them with tribute. After spending the night, they marched out onto the Iztapalapa Causeway, which led into the capital. Bernal Díaz in his *Historia Verdadera* recalled the scene:

> We went ahead on our causeway which is eight paces wide and goes directly to the city of Mexico without deviation. The whole width was so full of people that there was hardly room, some were going to Mexico, and others were leaving. We could hardly get through because the Indians who came to see us filled the towers and *cúes* [temples] and came in canoes from every part of the lake. And it was not surprising because they had never seen horses, nor men like us. And when we saw such wonderful things we did not know what to say, or whether what we saw before us was real. On the land there were great cities, and on the lake many more. We saw the whole lake was filled with canoes, and at intervals on the causeway there were many bridges. Before us was the

great city of Mexico. We had barely 400 soldiers, and we remembered the words and advice given us by the people of Guaxocinco [Huexotinco] and Tlaxcala and Tamanalco, and many others that we should beware of entering Mexico, because they would kill us once they had us inside.

Cacama and the other princes had gone ahead to prepare for the meeting between Cortés and Motecuhzoma. The emperor himself arrived on a litter with his brother, Cuitláhuac, prince of Iztapalapa, and Cacama on either side. Two hundred other princes formed the entourage, all of whom averted their eyes for they were forbidden to look at Motecuhzoma's face. A carpet was rolled out and Motecuhzoma stepped down on it, the two princes holding up his hands, while attendants swept in front of him so that dust would not touch his feet. Cortés started to embrace him, but the princes indicated that this was impossible. They did, however, allow him to take a necklace from his own neck, made of glass beads scented with musk, interspersed with pearls, and put it around the emperor's. Motecuhzoma summoned a servant, who brought a packet which the emperor opened. It contained a necklace made of red snail shells, interspersed with golden shrimp, which the emperor personally placed around Cortés's neck, to the astonishment of his retainers. After an exchange of pleasantries, Motecuhzoma ordered Cacama and the prince of Iztapalapa to show the Spaniards to their quarters.

The Itzapalapa Causeway led into the very center of the city which – then and now – is the administrative and spiritual center. It opened out onto a great plaza, now known as the Zócalo where crowds still gather for events and festivities of national importance. To the immediate east of the plaza was the palace of Motecuhzoma himself, now the site of the National Palace. North of the plaza were the temple precincts, now partly covered by the Metropolitan Cathedral, across from which are the ruins of the Great Temple itself. The Spaniards were quartered in the palace of Motecuhzoma's father, Axayacatl, the site of which is to the immediate west of the Cathedral, and the immediate north of the modern Monte de Piedad (National Pawn Shop). Just north of this palace was the Tlacopán or Tacuba Causeway, which was to figure prominently in subsequent events.

Motecuhzoma was waiting in Axayacatl's palace when the Spaniards arrived. Taking Cortés by the hand, the emperor led him to a throne, then took another next to it. Gifts of gold, silver, featherwork, and fine cotton garments were brought in. Then Motecuhzoma began to explain his people's history, explaining that the Aztecs themselves were foreigners who had been brought to the region by a great chieftain. When that chieftain wanted to move on, however, the Aztecs had refused. The chieftain left for the east, but the Aztecs had always known that his descendants would return to rule over them. Now, it appeared the prophecy had been fulfilled. "And in all the land that lies in my domain, you may command as you will, for you shall be obeyed; and for all that we own is for you to dispose of as you choose," he said. He also mentioned that

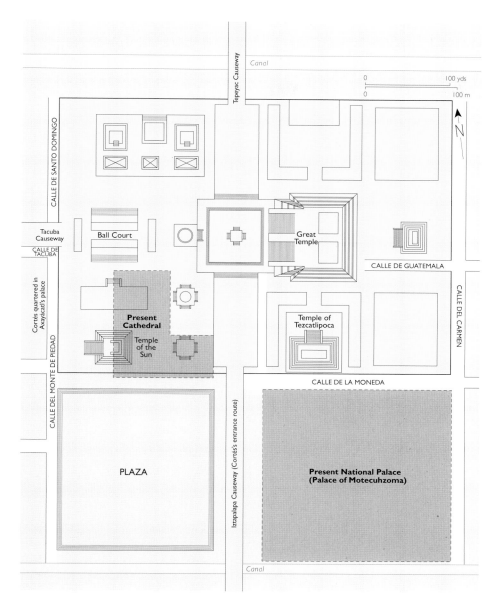

Precinct of the Great Temple
in Tenochtitlán.

he knew the stories about him that the Tlaxcalteca, Totonacs, and others had told, and cautioned Cortés not to take them too seriously. After telling the Spaniards to make themselves at home, he departed.

The Spaniards immediately set about organizing company quarters, siting their artillery, and assigning posts for infantry and cavalry. Once that was completed, they found the Mexicans had prepared a sumptuous banquet, and they ate it immediately. "And this," Bernal Díaz wrote, "was our daring and auspicious entrance into the great city of Tenustitán [Tenochtitlán] Mexico, on the eighth day of the month of November, in the year of Our Savior Jesus Christ one thousand five hundred and nineteen. Thanks to Our Lord Jesus Christ for it all."

THE FIGHTING

Acclimatization

For the next week, the Spaniards were tourists. They were well housed and well fed, acquiring a taste for strange new things, such as chocolate (derived from the Nahuatl word *xocolatl*) whipped to a froth, corn tortillas, and chilis. Often they dined with the emperor, who entertained them with dancers, jugglers, and jesters, and introduced them to smoking after dinner. They saw the menagerie, with strange native animals such as the beautiful quetzal bird, whose long plumes adorned the headdresses of royalty, jaguars, and coyotes (which Bernal Díaz thought were jackals). Particularly repulsive to the European mind was a type of snake "that had on its tail something that sounds like bells," their first introduction to the rattlesnake. Writing of the menagerie

The great Aztec calendar stone on display at the Museum of Anthropology, Mexico City. (Topfoto/The Image Works)

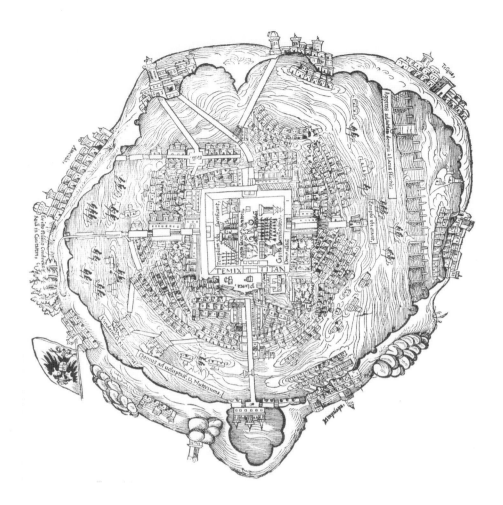

Albrecht Dürer's plan of the city of Tenochtitlán, attributed to Cortés, and first published in Nuremberg in 1524. Despite the European conventions in the rendering, it is surprisingly accurate, detailing the main ceremonial temples and main causeways. (American Museum of Natural History)

with particular disgust, Díaz contended these animals were fed with the hearts and flesh of sacrificial victims.

They also saw the Great Temple, a massive pyramid surmounted by twin sanctuaries, dedicated to Huitzilopochtli, the peculiarly Aztec war god, and Tlaloc, the multi-fanged, goggle-eyed god of rain, passed down through millennia from one Mesoamerican culture to the next. Inside the dark sanctuaries were the idols which, according to Andrés Tapia, were smeared with blood to the depth of two or three fingers.

In front of the Temple was the *tzompantli*, the great rack where the heads of sacrificial victims were threaded on beams set between towers. The towers themselves also were made of skulls mortared together. Visiting the *tzompantli*, Tapia and Gonzalo de Umbría did some idle counting and multiplication, and determined there were 136,000 skulls on the beams themselves, not including those in the towers.

On the fourth day, Motecuhzoma invited the Spaniards to accompany him to Tlatelolco, the commercial center of the empire. Although Aztec, Tlatelolco had established its independence early in the Aztec era, and remained separate until 1473,

FOLLOWING PAGES
A colonial Indian depiction of the Templo Mayor (Great Temple) and the *tzompantli* (skull rack). The Spaniards found the temple imposing and regarded the sacrificial practices as repugnant. (Courtesy of the John Carter Brown Library at Brown University)

Templo del ydolo Vitzilo
puchtli.

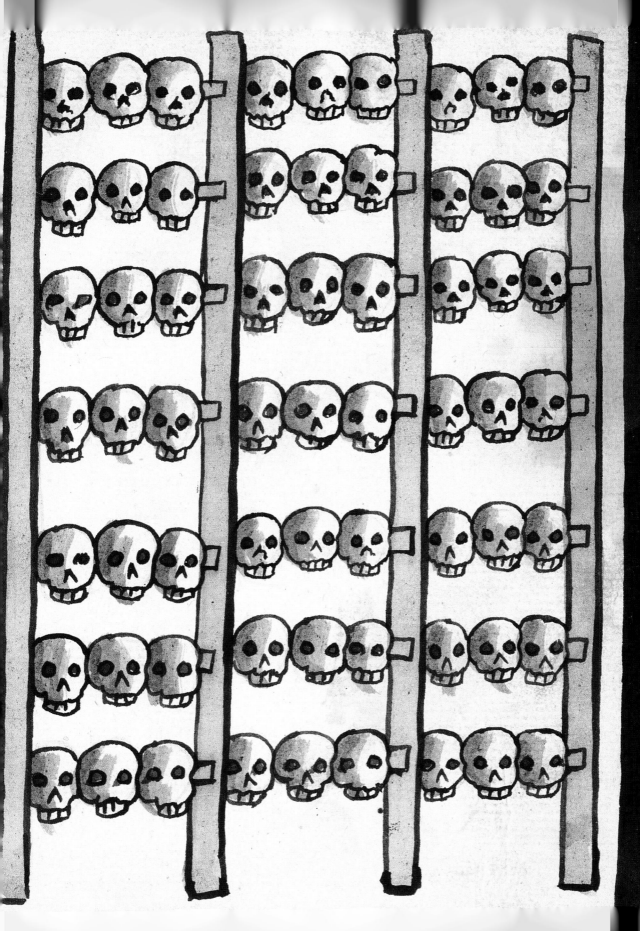

when Motecuhzoma's father, the Emperor Axyacatl, conquered it and made it into a borough of Tenochtitlán proper. Nevertheless, Tlatelolco maintained control of commerce, and had its own Great Temple complex, rivaling that of Mexico.

The vast market square, which virtually every Spanish chronicler agreed was more than double the size of the great square of Salamanca, was surrounded by a portico (the whole area was roughly 500ft square). Everyday, at least 20,000 people were trading, and on the main market day, every fifth day, this number more than doubled. Each type of trade had its own area, with the gold merchants in one, featherworkers in another, stoneworkers in another, slave dealers, traders in cotton, produce, game animals, medicinal roots, and every other imaginable item in its own area. Currency was feather quills filled with gold dust of a specific weight, or cacao beans. Some of the Spanish veterans, who had traveled as far as Constantinople, said they had never seen so large a market, nor one so well regulated.

Looming over the market was the Great Temple of Tlatelolco. Bernal Díaz counted 114 steps up the pyramid, from the top of which they could see the entire city. There were three causeways into the city from the mainland, with bridges at regular intervals. There was an aqueduct that brought in fresh water from springs at Chapultepec. The city itself was divided by canals traversed by drawbridge or canoe. In view of later events, one may surmise that Cortés noted everything, and committed it all to memory.

At Cortés's request, Motecuhzoma led them inside the sanctuary, dominated by an image of Huitzilopochtli, along with statues of Tezcatlipoca, the paramount god, and Xipe Totec, the flayed god of harvest. Díaz noted that,

> All the walls of that oratory were bathed and black with encrusted blood, and the floors were the same, and it stank dreadfully, to which the butchers of Castile could not compare. And there had they offered five hearts sacrificed that day... They had a drum great in dimension, that when they beat it, it had a mournful sound of the style they say one hears from an instrument of the infernal regions, and one can hear it from two leagues distant; they say the drumheads are made from the skins of great serpents.
>
> And in that place they had various things diabolical to see: bugles and trumpets and sacrificial knives, and many hearts of Indians had been burned to fumigate those idols, and the whole was such that I curse it, and it was clotted with blood, and stank like a slaughterhouse, and we could not wait until we left that stink and that horrible sight.

Turning to the emperor, Cortés said he could not understand how such a great and wise prince could not have realized that these were not gods but demons. In order that he and his priests might truly understand the nature of the idols, he asked to place a cross on top of the sanctuary, and inside, a statue of the Virgin "so that you may see the fear the idols have of her."

As this was translated, two priests glared malevolently, and Motecuhzoma angrily replied, "Lord Malinche, if I had believed that you would speak with such dishonor to my gods, I would not have brought you here. We have them because they are good, and they give us health, and rains, and good plantings and seasons, and victories when we want them, and we are required to worship and to sacrifice. And we pray that you do not say further words in their dishonor."

Smiling, Cortés suggested it was time to leave. Motecuhzoma agreed, but replied that he would have to stay, and pray and make sacrifices to ask pardon of the gods for bringing the Spaniards. Cortés then said, "I ask my lord's pardon if this be so."

The emperor, however, was less intractable with regard to how the Spaniards worshiped among themselves, and gave permission to set up a chapel in their quarters. As a room was being surveyed, the carpenter noticed a doorway that had recently been bricked up and plastered over. Cortés ordered the door forced open. Inside was a vast chamber containing the accumulated wealth of conquest and empire. After a quick conference between Cortés and the men present, it was decided to seal the door again, so that Motecuhzoma would not realize it had been discovered.

Imprisonment of Motecuhzoma

Cortés and some of the more experienced captains and soldiers were worried. Fabulous as it was, the treasure had impressed them with the might and power of the Aztec empire. They were beginning to see the city as a trap. Motecuhzoma could stop their food and water, raise the bridges, then set hordes of warriors on them. Their fears seemed confirmed when runners from the coast brought word of a rebellion, instigated by the Mexicans, against the garrison at Villa Rica. The Tlaxcalteca also reported that Motecuhzoma planned to raise the bridges in the city. Cortés decided the time had come to act. Taking a squad of armed soldiers, he called on the emperor, accused him of treachery, and placed him under arrest. Motecuhzoma argued for an hour but, overpowered by the personality of Cortés, and with a not-too-veiled threat from Doña Marina, he acquiesced, and was conveyed back to the Spanish quarters in Axayacatl's palace. The population was given to understand that Motecuhzoma had taken up residence there, and Cortés allowed the usual functions of government to continue, but under guard and with Doña Marina always listening.

On the summons of Motecuhzoma, Cualpopoca, the Mexican governor of the Pánuco region, who had instigated the uprising, was summoned to Mexico. Arriving about mid-December on a rich litter attended by his sons and 15 nobles, Cualpopoca was arrested, and together with his entourage, was handed over to Cortés, who ordered them interrogated under torture. They confessed, and implicated Motecuhzoma. They were burned at the stake in the great square, where López de Gómara wrote that the local population watched silently, too terrified to interfere. Cortés ordered Motecuhzoma chained.

It was increasingly obvious that Motecuhzoma was completely cowed by the Spaniards. Others, however, were not. Chief among them was Cacama, king of Texcoco, the second

Charles V and the Americas

With the death of King Ferdinand in 1516, both the Aragonese crown and the Castilian regency passed to his grandson, a 16-year-old-boy named Charles, who had been brought up in Flanders. Upon arriving in a country he had never seen, whose customs he did not understand, and whose various languages he could not speak, he insisted not simply upon being the regent for Castile, but to share its crown. Thus, the first king of a united Spain was a foreigner who inaugurated the Spanish branch of an Austrian dynasty, the Habsburgs.

Charles was short and pale. No portrait, however flattering, could conceal the long jaw and protruding lower lip that came to define the Habsburgs. Even in languages he knew, his speech was so slow as to be almost incoherent, in short he was a far cry from the rugged warrior kings that had dominated Castilian history and that Spaniards almost demanded.

Charles found in Spain a country eking out a subsistence living, and an austere court. Although this austerity bred the Conquistadores, who ultimately would win him an empire beyond imagination, the sole imperial resources at this point were a few islands in the West Indies that brought virtually nothing and which were of little interest to the new king.

In early 1519, he learned that his grandfather Maximilian had died, initiating a scramble for the vacant imperial throne of the Holy Roman Empire. Among the chief contenders were his uncle by marriage, Henry VIII, and Francis I of France. Determined to win at all costs, Charles bribed the electors on an unprecedented scale and won the crown, creating huge debts that Spain was expected to help absorb. Charles I of Spain was now Charles V of the Holy Roman Empire. Henceforth there would be long periods of absentee rule while the king-emperor tended to his German holdings. For the next two centuries the interests of Spain would often be subordinated to the interests of the Habsburg family in central Europe. Spain, however, would shoulder the economic burden, frittering away much of the vast riches won by Cortés and others.

In the fall of 1519, Charles toured his Spanish dominions, which were now on the verge of rebellion. Grievances included the unanticipated debt, the consolidation of the monarchy, ignorance of Spanish customs and traditions by the king-emperor's Flemish appointees, and Charles's determination to depart for Germany the following year to accept the imperial crown. Amid this internal turmoil, Francisco de Montejo and Alonso Hernández de Puertocarrero arrived in Seville to press Hernán Cortés's case, bringing with them the first shipload of treasure from Mexico, and the delegation of Totonac Indians. Their ship and funds were impounded, and the treasure was deposited with the Casa de Contratación, the royal appraisal office that was responsible for the Indies, from whence Charles ordered it turned over to the keeper of the crown jewels.

CARLOS V

Charles was anxious to leave Spain. Stung by the resentment of his Spanish subjects, he was even more concerned that his newly won suzerainty over Germany was crumbling. Nevertheless, as he hurried through Spain travelling to the port of Corunna on the north coast and thence to Germany, he found time to invite Cortés's ambassadors Montejo and Puertocarrero to court. They presented him with a petition calling for the recognition of the Cortés expedition as an official expedition of conquest, for release of its funds and ship, and for the supplies so urgently needed. On March 3, 1521, the treasures were displayed in court, and the Totonacs presented to the king and the *Cortes* the Castilian parliament. (The Spanish word *Cortes*, without the accented "e" means court; *Cortés* translates as "courteous.") Charles was particularly fascinated with the Indians, whom he ordered treated with extreme consideration.

However, Montejo and Puertocarrero were not the only representatives of the New World at court. En route back to Seville, they had stopped to reprovision in Cuba, where Diego Velásquez learned of the vast treasure on board the ship. In April 1519, his deputy, Pánfilo de Narváez, had returned from Spain with a license for Velásquez to conquer Yucatán and what was dimly understood to be Mexico. Now, learning that Cortés had beaten him to it, he dispatched Narváez on his ill-fated mission to end the Cortés expedition, and also held hearings, assembled evidence, and dispatched deputies to Spain to present his case.

Velásquez's representatives countered Montejo and Puertocarrero arguing that, far from being a loyal subject, Cortés was little more than a pirate and traitor. It was a wasted effort. Swayed, no doubt, by the treasure, the *Cortes* agreed to postpone any final decision between the two until both could be heard (and to wait and see whether Cortés succeeded or failed). The councilors even went so far as to suggest that Velásquez might do better by bringing a civil suit. Even more important, the ship was released, along with the money from Mexico for use as the Cortés adherents saw fit, specifically to purchase the necessary supplies. A few days later, the king departed for Germany. The Totonacs, who were beginning to suffer from the climate of northern Spain, were sent back to Seville. One died and the others ultimately were sent back to the Americas, although it appears they got no further than Cuba.

The Cortés expedition was not the only overseas venture on the king's mind. He had been persuaded to sponsor an expedition under Ferdinand Magellan, a Portuguese in Spanish service, which departed Spain in 1519 with five ships in an effort to fulfill Columbus's vision of reaching the East Indies by sailing west. Magellan discovered a passage around South America, sailed across the Pacific and arrived in the Philippines in 1521. Here he was killed in a fight with natives. His lieutenant, Juan Sebastián del Cano, continued the voyage, arriving back in Spain with one ship and 18 men. Although del Cano received a coat of arms and pension for being the first man to sail around the world, Charles V barely recovered his costs, further dampening his already marginal interest in exploration and conquest.

It seemed that Charles could never escape the changes that the New World unleashed on his own inflexible world. Columbus's discoveries had brought into question thousands of years of accumulated knowledge. Not only had he found an unknown continent, but that continent contained people. Columbus, envisioning himself as Christopher, the Bearer of Christ, had expected to encounter Asians, recognized as humans with immortal souls and therefore candidates for salvation. The Indians of the New World, however, had been isolated for millennia from the mainstream of world affairs. They were unlike anyone known by the people of the Old World. This raised the question of whether they were even human, or instead some highly developed species of animal, capable of profound mimicry, architecture, and manual skill. Assuming they were human (which many Europeans were unwilling to concede), some Conquistadores regarded them as a subspecies, incapable of civilization or salvation. Therefore, in the view of the settlers, they were open to exploitation and abuse.

Yet there were those who insisted the Indians were children of God and must be treated as such. Among the most militant of these was Bartolomé de las Casas. Las Casas had come to the Indies in 1502. He was the classic adventurer-speculator, acquiring mines and estates where he relentlessly worked his Indian slaves. He was an enthusiastic participant in the vicious conquest of Cuba, and was rewarded with more estates and slaves. In 1514, however, the 40-year-old las Casas experienced a profound revelation concerning the atrocities he and his countrymen were inflicting on the Indians, and he devoted the remainder of his 92 years to being their champion.

Returning to Spain, las Casas met with Charles V, who, persuaded by his arguments, authorized the establishment of Indian utopian communities on the Venezuelan coast. This plan failed and las Casas retreated to Santo Domingo, where he began work on a vast treatise, part history, part prophecy, and part fabrication. Entitled *Brevísimia relación de la destrucción de las Indias* (A Very Brief Account of the Destruction of the Indies), it saw wide circulation throughout Europe. Translated (with embellishments) into English and Dutch, it formed the basis of the infamous "Black Legend" of Spanish atrocities that haunts relations between the English-speaking and Spanish-speaking worlds to this day.

On trips to Spain over the ensuing years, las Casas would continue to advise Charles. His discussion with the king-emperor got an additional boost in 1537, when Pope Paul III issued the bull *Sublimis Deus*, which proclaimed Indians to be children of God worthy of salvation. Charles's contribution was a legal code known as the New Laws that regulated conquest and colonization, tempered subjugation with salvation, and attempted to end exploitation by, among other things, the abolition of the encomiendas, an effort that was only partially successful. Nevertheless, las Casas is still respected throughout Central America, and is one of the very few Spaniards honored in Mexico, as the "Apostle of the Indies." (Image of Charles V from Museo Nacional de Historia, Mexico)

partner in the Aztec Triple Alliance. Initially, he had urged Motecuhzoma to resist the Spaniards, and when it became obvious he would not, he decided the time had come to seize power and expel the foreigners. He was joined in the conspiracy by Motecuhzoma's brother, Cuitláhuac, prince of Itzapalapa, and several of the other more important vassal states in the Valley of Mexico. Motecuhzoma learned of the plot, and by now completely in thrall to Cortés, arranged for some of the still-loyal nobles to seize Cacama and bring him to Mexico, where he was turned over to the Spaniards and placed under arrest. Cortés deposed him, replacing him as king of Texcoco with his brother, Coanacoch.

So far, Cortés had managed the expedition without a single serious error. Now, however, he overreached himself. Wily and sophisticated as he was, he was nevertheless driven partly by his religious convictions and believed that the time had come to throw down the idols of Tenochtitlán, end the sacrifices and impose the rule of the Catholic Church. With a hand-picked squad he crossed the compound to the Great Temple of Mexico, and climbed the steps of the pyramid. Reaching the platform, the soldiers drew their swords and slashed through a heavy curtain decorated with bells that hid the sanctuary. The racket brought the priests running and found Cortés inside, looking at the blood-soaked idols and muttering "Oh God! Why do You permit such great honor paid the Devil in this land? Look with favor, Lord, upon our service to You here."

Turning to the priests, he told them the gods would be replaced by a statue of the Virgin and Child and the walls would be whitewashed. They laughed and replied that these were gods not only of the city, but of the entire empire. The people were willing to die for them, and upon seeing the Spaniards mount the pyramid, some already began preparations for a rebellion. Angered, Cortés sent one of the men back to the palace to strengthen the guard around Motecuhzoma and send a detail of 30 or 40 men to the Temple. Then, as Andrés Tapia recalled:

> On my faith as a gentleman I swear by God that, as I recall it now, the *marqués* [Cortés] leaped supernaturally, and, balancing himself by gripping the bar in the middle, he reached as high as the idol's eyes and thus tore down the gold masks, saying: "Something we must venture for the Lord."

Motecuhzoma suspected what was about to happen, and demanded to be taken to the temple, where he confronted Cortés. Now it was the emperor's turn for subtlety, and he suggested that the Spaniards leave the idols undisturbed, and erect a cross and the religious statues next to the Mexican gods. Cortés, meanwhile, had overcome his initial outrage and agreed, saying the idols were nothing but stone and therefore unimportant. However, he demanded the temple be cleansed and whitewashed, and the sacrifices end.

The violation of their gods was more than the people were willing to tolerate. The priests, seeing a threat to their massive power, spread the word that the two great gods,

OPPOSITE
A statue of Tlaloc, the old Teotihuacán-Tollan storm god, dating from around AD 400, and now situated at the Museo Nacional de Antropologia, Mexico. (© Philip Baird, www.anthroarcheart.org)

The main pyramid at Cempoala was the scene of pivotal events of the Conquest, including the first alliance with native states, the first overthrow of the native idols, and Cortés's defeat of a rival expedition sent from Cuba under Pánfilo de Narváez. (Instituo Nacional de Antropologia e Historia, Mexico)

Huitzilopochtli and Tezcatlipoca, would abandon Mexico unless Christian symbols were removed from the temple, and the Spaniards themselves destroyed. Cortés's page, Orteguilla, who had quickly learned Nahuatl, and to whom Motecuhzoma had taken a liking, reported that the emperor was quietly conferring with his generals. The Tlaxcalteca and Doña Marina also warned of an impending revolt. Even Motecuhzoma told Cortés that unless he evacuated his men and left the country, they would be destroyed.

Cortés now realized his diplomacy was spent, and he would have to hold the country by sheer force. He sent secret orders to the carpenters in Villa Rica to begin the construction of three ships to sail to the immediate Indies for reinforcements. Meanwhile, he stalled, telling Motecuhzoma that he and his men would like to return home, but were unable because they had no way of leaving the country. One day, however, Motecuhzoma advised him that he could now leave, because a fleet had anchored at Villa Rica. Cortés correctly surmised that this expedition came from Cuba, where Governor Velásquez had learned of his plans when the shipload of tribute had put in to reprovision for the trip back to Spain. He also knew that before Cualpopoca had instigated the uprising in the Pánuco, he had already expelled another expedition by Francisco de Garay, the governor of Jamaica.

Arrival of the Narváez expedition

The new expedition to Mexico was commanded by Pánfilo de Narváez, who had encountered one of Cortés's scouting parties, and learned of the situation in Mexico. Unable to occupy Villa Rica, where the tough, defiant captain Gonzalo Sandoval dug in

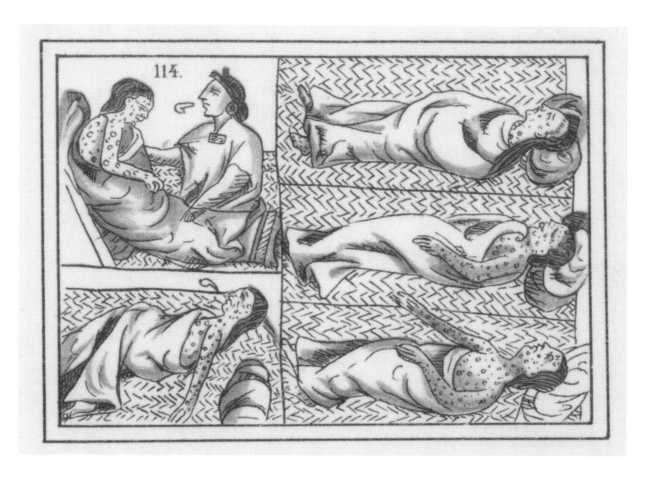

for a siege, Narváez bypassed the town and continued on to Cempoala, where he was now quartered with his troops. Sandoval had also arrested three of Narváez's envoys and sent them under guard to Mexico, where Cortés learned of his adversary's strength. Letters from Narváez, calling Cortés's men "bandits" and "traitors," and threatening them with death, were read out to the Spaniards in Mexico to stir them up against the newcomers. Then the envoys were sent back to Narváez, loaded with gifts and stories of the wealth and grandeur that Cortés offered, compared to their own lack of prospects with Narváez. Finally, Cortés set out for the coast with 250 picked men, leaving Pedro de Alvarado in command of the city.

There can be little doubt that the new arrivals were swayed by the gifts of gold and talk of riches. Yet one must also remember that they had only recently arrived from the comparative luxury of Cuba. No doubt they also would have noticed the lean, leathery countenances of Cortés's men, and their battered armor, and realized they would be facing battle-hardened veterans. The Narváez expedition was effectively defeated even before it fought.

The battle itself occurred at Cempoala on May 27, 1520. Cortés moved in before dawn in a driving rain, which his own men, accustomed to hardship, barely noticed, but

The *Florentine Codex* graphically depicts the effects of the smallpox epidemic that ravaged Tenochtitlán between October and December 1520, killing hundreds of thousands of Indian people, including the newly elected *huey tlatoani*, Cuitláhuac. (*Florentine Codex*, Bk 12, Ch. 29, American Museum of Natural History)

which drove Narváez's men under cover. The veterans quickly seized the artillery and unhorsed the cavalry, and rushed into the city. Much of the resistance came from the main temple, where Narváez fortified himself with crossbowmen and musketeers. They mounted a counterattack, but at that moment, Sandoval arrived with a detachment from the coast, and the combined forces pushed them back. Then the roof of the temple was set on fire, driving Narváez's men out. Narváez himself, badly wounded and having lost an eye in the fighting, was sent back to the coast as a prisoner. A detachment was sent to Villa Rica to remove the rudders, compasses, and sails of the ships, so they could not escape to Cuba. The bulk of Narváez's men, having accepted a pardon from Cortés, were rearmed and incorporated into the army.

As he prepared to return to Mexico, Cortés little realized he was leaving behind an unexpected and invisible ally that would have devastating consequences for the native people. An African slave attached to Narváez's men had smallpox, and infected the household where he was quartered in Cempoala. As López de Gómara noted, "it spread from one Indian to another, and they, being so numerous and eating and sleeping together, quickly infected the whole country."

The people of the Old World, over hundreds of generations and perhaps millions of deaths, had built a resistance to the disease. The genetically weak died off; the genetically strong recovered and procreated descendants with enhanced immune systems. The people of the New World had never experienced smallpox and had no inherited immunity. It is estimated that as much as 90 percent of the entire native population of the New World ultimately died of diseases introduced after Columbus.

In modern times, the science of microbiology has diminished the impact of disease and it is impossible for the 21st-century imagination to truly comprehend the impact of a pandemic. The elders die before they can impart their accumulated wisdom. The priests, philosophers, and political leaders die, taking with them their belief structure, knowledge, and governmental institutions. Craftsmen, farmers, and warriors die. Children are orphaned. Often the dead outnumber the living, and the streets are filled with decaying corpses, exacerbating the crisis. Society quite simply collapses. As much as any other factor, this new and unknown plague would decide the outcome of the Conquest.

The Toxcatl massacre

While Cortés was dealing with Narváez, Alvarado had problems of his own back in Mexico. May, which the Aztecs called Toxcatl, was sacred to Huitzilopochtli, and the occasion of great festivals, during which a proxy for the god was sacrificed. Alvarado gave permission for the celebration on condition that the Christian symbols in the temple were not disturbed, and there would be no sacrifices. A few days before the ceremony was to begin, however, he inspected the temple, found fresh sacrifices, and slaves awaiting their turn. Freeing the slaves, he arrested several priests who, on interrogation, admitted arms were stored in the temple precincts, and confessed that on the completion of the ceremony, the Spanish guards would be overwhelmed and the cross thrown down as the

OPPOSITE
Pedro de Alvarado (1485–1541). Headstrong and impulsive, Alvarado may have provoked the uprising in the city of Mexico by overreacting. Nevertheless, in any crisis, he was valiant, decisive, and loyal to the end. (Topfoto)

FOLLOWING PAGES
The Temple of the Sun at Teotihuacán, seen here from a ceremonial complex known as the "Citadel," was already ancient when the Aztecs first arrived in the Valley of Mexico as semi-barbaric nomads. They made this temple the center of their world, and the mythical point of their origin. (© Philip Baird, www.anthroarcheart.org)

signal for an uprising. It would be all the easier because the city was filled with pilgrims who were outraged at the sight of the cross on the temple and by its foreign guards.

Alvarado waited for the ceremony to begin on May 18, then, leaving part of his troops in the palace, he took the rest into the temple compound, pushing his way through the crowd. The procession of priests parted to reveal armed warriors, but Alvarado was expecting this, and his men charged. Ignoring the rank and file, they went for the nobles and warlords, slaughtering the leadership and leaving the masses of warriors in confusion. Meanwhile, about 1,000 Tlaxcalteca surrounded the temple court and held off reinforcements. Together, Alvarado and the Tlaxcalteca fought their way back to the palace, leaving the compound littered with corpses and drenched in blood.

Couriers brought word to Cortés that the city was in rebellion, Alvarado was under siege, and by now in danger of collapse. He rushed his newly strengthened army back through Tlaxcala, picking up several thousand more auxiliaries. The closer he came to the capital, the more signs he saw of rebellion. There were no welcoming delegations and the people were sullen. A quiet reigned over the city as the force arrived on the evening of June 24. There were accusations and counter-accusations between Alvarado and Motecuhzoma. Cortés tended to believe Motecuhzoma's account, and Alvarado received a thorough dressing-down. Nevertheless, Motecuhzoma also received his share of wrath, because Cortés had learned the emperor had been conspiring secretly with Narváez.

The arguments quickly became academic because the Mexicans renewed the siege. Hordes of warriors rushed the palace, their sheer numbers rendering artillery, musket fire, and crossbows ineffective. Dozens dropped with every charge, but still more came, forcing their way into the palace and setting it on fire in several places. Finally, they were pushed back by sword point. The Spaniards next built siege towers in an effort to capture some of the surrounding buildings that Mexican slingers and archers were using as vantage points. When these failed, Cortés led a raiding party that captured and burned the temple, although the Christian images had already been removed by the Aztecs themselves. After that he began leading parties out into the city to burn the surrounding buildings. Nevertheless, it was becoming obvious that ultimately the Aztecs would prevail by sheer numbers. Almost every soldier was wounded in some way. In the midst of the fighting, the Aztec electors deposed Motecuhzoma, and named Cuitláhuac emperor.

Late in the siege Motecuhzoma died, although the exact cause will never be known. Cortés contended that the former emperor went out to address the crowd in an effort to end the fighting. When he reached a breastworks he was struck on the head by a stone, and died of the injury three days later. The Aztecs, however, told a different story. Durán's informants said the wound from the stone had healed, and that he was murdered by the Spaniards. Sahagún was told that Motecuhzoma did address the crowd, which only infuriated them more. After that, Cortés decided he was a liability, and ordered him garroted along with several other nobles, and the bodies thrown down from the roof of the palace.

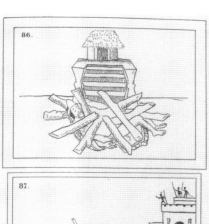

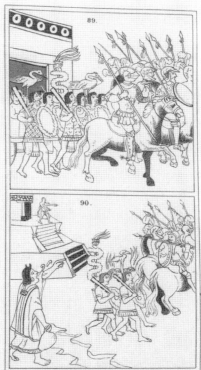

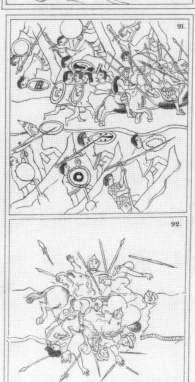

This page of the *Florentine Codex* illustrates some of the events of 1520. The second illustration down on the right illustrates an Aztec legend related to *La Noche Triste*, when the army was spotted by a woman drawing water, and she warned the watch at the Temple of Huitzilopochtli. The illustrations below chart the ensuing battle. (*Florentine Codex*, Bk 12, Ch 24, American Museum of Natural History)

FOLLOWING PAGES
During *La Noche Triste*, the Spaniards and their Tlaxcaltecan allies found themselves trapped on the Tlacopán causeway. Using canoes, the Aztecs attacked from all sides, and score of men were driven into the canals where they drowned. (Plate 18, *Lienzo de Tlaxcala*, American Museum of Natural History)

The native version of events, that the emperor was murdered by the Spaniards, tends to be accepted by historians of the modern, post-colonial era. Yet the fact is that virtually every Conquistador account upholds Cortés, and some of these soldiers-turned-writers had no particular reason for doing so unless it was the truth. The two most convincing are Alonso de Aguilar, and Bernal Díaz. When Aguilar wrote his memoir, he was past 80, and living in menial servitude as a Dominican under the religious name of Fra Francisco, in an apparent effort to atone for his own atrocities during the Conquest. He stated that Motecuhzoma died of the head injury, although he admits that Cortés had the other prisoners murdered. Díaz, who admired Motecuhzoma, wrote that after he was stoned by the crowd, the emperor became despondent, refusing food and medical treatment. Considering that Motecuhzoma had been assaulted by a population which only recently had considered him a demigod, Díaz's scenario is most believable, although his remark that the Spaniards wept over his death is, at the very least, an exaggeration.

By June 30, with the siege six days old, the leading captains and the rank and file realized their position in the city was untenable. If they remained, they would be massacred. When Cortés demurred, the captains, including the normally loyal Alvarado brothers, came as close to mutiny as they ever would during the Conquest, informing him that he could either lead them out or stay behind. Accepting the inevitable, Cortés agreed and began laying plans for a retreat that would commence at midnight that very night.

Until this point, Cortés had proved a master of diplomacy and campaign strategy, learning to play indigenous factions against one another in order to achieve his goals with a minimum commitment of his own resources. He seemed to have had a remarkable aptitude for grasping the nature of each political situation and being ready to confront his opponents with both masterful acts of benevolence on the one hand, and sheer treachery on the other. His tactics were ultimately derived from the notable successes of Spain's monarchs during the conquest of Granada, when they engineered the virtual collapse of the emirate by pitting three pretenders against one another prior to any actual commitment of military forces. King Ferdinand himself, it was said, had even been the inspiration for Machiavelli's *The Prince*.

While Motecuhzoma's seizure had been a bold maneuver, it was not without precedent in either Europe or the Spanish Main. Medieval princes were notorious for seizing royal hostages either for ransom or to effect a more favorable political situation within the captive's own domain. Conquistadores like Velásquez and Ponce de León had achieved their ends with the seizure and outrageous executions of *caciques* (local kings) by having them burned alive. In 1513 Núñez de Balboa succeeded in capturing the *cacique* Tubanama in Panama and holding him hostage until his people had paid 90lb of gold. Emulating his success 20 years later, Pizarro seized the emperor Atahualpa and forced the Inca people to commit tons of gold and silver to secure his release. On June 30, 1520, Cortés was about to confront an entirely new situation. If the Aztec imperial army had been unable to take to the field before, it would never hesitate again.

veyotlipan.

Breakout and retreat

It was at this point that Aguilar reports Motecuhzoma's death, and Cortés ordered the slaughter of the remaining chiefs. Then, with nothing more to gain by concealment, the great treasure room was broken open, and about eight tons of gold, silver, and gems parceled out. One-fifth went to the Crown, according to law, and one-fifth to Cortés himself, according to the old agreement back in Villa Rica, by which he "accepted" the position to which the men "appointed" him. The bulk of this was melted down and turned into ingots for ease of transportation. Seven wounded war horses and a mare, along with 80 Tlaxcaltecan bearers were provided for the king's share. Once these formalities were completed, the rest was turned over to the men in a free-for-all. The bulk of it was grabbed by the Narváez men, while most of Cortés's veterans contented themselves with small, light gemstones or other trinkets that weighed little. Unlike the newcomers, they knew what they were up against, and that, with or without treasure, they would be very lucky to come out alive. Bales of quetzal feathers, priceless to the Indians, were distributed among the Tlaxcalteca.

The *Lienzo de Tlaxcala* portrays Cortés presenting the *matlaxopilli*, or net-bird claw signal banner, that he seized at the battle of Otumba to Lord Maxixcatzin. The Tlaxcalteca in turn offered the Spaniards food and shelter in preparation for a new assault on the Aztec imperial capital. (*Lienzo de Tlaxcala*, American Museum of Natural History)

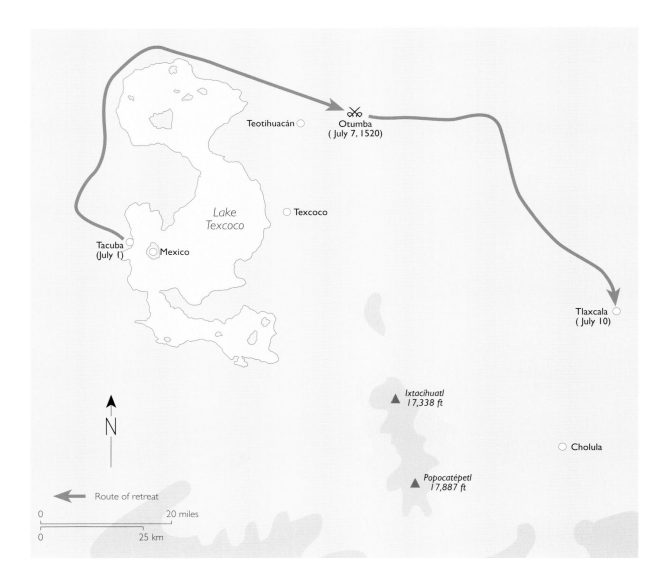

Teotihuacán ○
Otumba
(July 7, 1520)

Lake Texcoco

○ Texcoco

Tacuba
(July 1)
○ Mexico

Tlaxcala ○
(July 10)

▲ *Ixtacíhuatl*
17,338 ft

○ Cholula

▲ *Popocatépetl*
17,887 ft

N

← Route of retreat

0 ——————— 20 miles
0 ——————— 25 km

The Spanish retreat after *La Noche Triste*. The fighting occurred on the causeways leading from Tenochtitlán to Tacuba and the remnants of the army retreated north.

Carpenters ripped out beams from the palace, and put together a portable bridge to throw over the gaps in the causeway. At midnight, the long line of Spaniards and Indian auxiliaries filed out along the Tacuba Causeway. The weather turned ugly and a rainstorm broke, driving many of the Mexican sentries under cover. Then came one of those freak occurrences that so often change the course of events. According to some sources, a woman left her home to draw water, saw them, and gave the alarm. According to others, it was a sentry. Either way, within minutes, the great temple drum sounded, stirring the city to action. Warriors swarmed onto the causeway, and more came up alongside in canoes. The Mexicans' loathing of the Spaniards was so strong that they seem to have ignored their usual mode of war, and attempted to kill rather than capture their enemies. In his own picturesque style, Bernal Díaz recalled them shouting, "Oh, villains, do you still live?" Aguilar wrote of the battle:

Francis I of France

Charles V's chief rival in Europe was Francis I of France. Like Charles, Francis was young — barely out of his teens — and the first of a new dynasty. But where Charles's interest in Spain and the Indies was secondary compared to his concern over Germany, Francis was entirely devoted to French aggrandizement. He aspired to control the rich mercantile region of northern Italy, splitting Charles's domains in half, and making France the dominant power in Europe. Physically no two men could have been more dissimilar. Francis was an outdoorsman, a skilled hunter, an excellent rider, and an accomplished wrestler. Well developed mentally as well as physically, he was the epitome of style and sophistication in a country that increasingly viewed itself as the center of cultural patronage and refinement. What France might lack, Francis provided by importing artistic geniuses like Leonardo da Vinci and Benvenuto Cellini. His portraits, the most famous of which is the oversized masterpiece by Jean Clouet now hanging in the Louvre, show a handsome, shrewd, self-confident man with a trace of smugness.

Following Columbus's first voyage, the papacy had brokered a series of treaties aimed at quelling the rivalry between the Spaniards and Portuguese as to who should control the Indies trade. By the Treaty of Tordesillas in 1494 Portugal was given dominion over all territory east of the treaty line (sited some 370 miles west of the Azores), and the Spaniards received everything to the west. The overseas commerce of other nations, such as England and France, was negligible, and the possibility that they might involve themselves never occurred to anyone. With the accession of Francis to the French throne, however, this changed. Resenting Spain's claim to monopoly in the New World, he was determined to get his share.

In 1523, with Mexico firmly in Spanish hands, a fleet departed for Seville loaded with treasure, New World produce, and exotic animals, the first major payoff of the Conquest. Approaching Cape St. Vincent, the ships were waylaid by French corsairs who seized 700lb of pearls, 500lb of gold dust, and cases of gold and silver ingots. The French had sailed under royal patronage, and Francis received ample share of the plunder. Henceforth, the French not only waylaid homebound Spanish ships (the so-called "Treasure Fleets"), but cruised the Indies, attacking commerce, and trading with settlers in violation of Spain's royal monopoly. When Charles complained to the pope, Francis countered, "The sun shines for me as for the Spaniard." (Image of Francis I, Topfoto/British Library/HIP)

Here many Spaniards fell, some dead and some wounded, and others without any injury who fainted away from fright. And since all of us were fleeing, there was not a man who would lift a hand to help his companion or even his own father, nor a brother his own brother.

Muskets and crossbows, useless in close quarters, were thrown aside as men relied on sword thrusts to get through. A rearguard with the baggage was cut off, and the men retreated up the steps of the temple for a last stand, where they were finally overpowered. Many of the Aztecs fell to plundering the baggage train, giving the remnants of the army a breather as it made its way across the lake to the safety of the mainland.

Modern authorities estimate Spanish losses to be at least 600, the bulk of the army, along with most of their horses and all their cannon. The Tlaxcaltecan loss was several thousand. The night of June 30/July 1, 1520 is known in Mexican history as *La Noche Triste*, "The Sad Night."

The battle of Otumba

The battered, beaten Spaniards struggled back toward Tlaxcala, marching north around Lake Texcoco and then turning east, more or less constantly harassed by skirmishers. Finally, the Mexicans decided to destroy them completely and finish the war. The place picked for the final blow was the plain of Otumba, near the sacred ruins of Teotihuacán where, it was presumed, their massed infantry, led by Tenochtitlán's high priest, would overwhelm the remnants of Cortés's army. In choosing this ground they committed a fatal error. Their firsthand experience with the great Andalusian war horses was within the city

and on the bridges, where the horses' iron-shod hooves slipped on the pavement, and their mobility was restricted. They had completely underestimated them, and now presented Cortés with the perfect situation for cavalry.

The battle, which was fought on July 7, was very close. According to Alonso de Aguilar, Cortés was in tears as he exhorted the men for one final effort. Recounting the struggle for King Charles, Cortés himself wrote, "We could hardly distinguish between ourselves and them, so fiercely and closely did they fight with us. Certainly we believed that it was our last day, for the Indians were very strong and we could resist but feebly, as we were exhausted and nearly all of us wounded and weak from hunger." Finally, Cortés spotted the group of warlords directing the battle and, lining up his lancers, led a mounted charge through the massed warriors, the horses breaking through the mass of warriors to the warlords. The senior chief was impaled on a lance and the Mexicans, on the verge of victory, lost their morale and began to retreat.

The army was saved, but was in no condition to do anything but continue on to Tlaxcala. Bernal Díaz estimated that besides the European losses on *La Noche Triste*, another 72 had died in the fighting since, along with five Spanish women who had come with Narváez. The heaviest losses, in fact, were among the Narváez men, who were unaccustomed to the life-or-death nature of the war, and to the discipline necessary to stay alive, and who had been weighted down with treasure on the bridges.

The Mexicans had already approached the Tlaxcalteca and asked them to put aside the old grievances and unite against the foreigners, and one faction in Tlaxcala was amenable. The senior lords, however, quelled this movement at its inception, determined to remain steadfast to Cortés, and warned of dire consequences against whoever sided with Mexico. Thus, when the exhausted, battered Spaniards arrived in Tlaxcala on July 10, they were greeted with the words, "This is your home, where you may rest and find pleasure after the hardships you have suffered."

The Conquest revived

Despite his defeat, Cortés was determined to go back, finish with Tenochtitlán, and subjugate the entire country. In this, he was backed by his old veterans. After sending to Villa Rica for more powder and arms, resting his men, and allowing them to recuperate from their wounds, he sent an expeditionary force of Spaniards and Tlaxcalteca to subjugate the city of Tepeaca, where the Mexican garrison met him on a plain and, as at Otumba, was cut to pieces by the cavalry. With this boost to morale, and with the discipline it instilled in the Narváez contingent, he moved again against various other Mexican towns, sacking some and frightening others into submission.

Having subjugated the entire province, Cortés founded the city Segura de la Frontera, to use as a base against Tenochtitlán. A complete administration was established, and buildings and fortifications erected in a remarkably short time. The site was chosen not only for its strategic position, but because the countryside was ideally suited for future settlement. As ever, Cortés was looking ahead. Some of his men were less enthusiastic,

OPPOSITE
These images from the *Florentine Codex* show the fighting in Tenochtitlán. As the battle for Tenochtitlán continued, certain soldiers on both sides began to emerge as heroic characters. The middle image on the right shows "Tzilacatzin the mighty." The Spaniards were especially fearful of this Otomi-class warrior who was known for carrying a shield loaded with huge wall stones that he hurled at their formations. (*Florentine Codex*, Bk 12, Ch.32, American Museum of Natural History)

and he had to quell a potential mutiny among some of the Narváez hardliners, hanging one of their ringleaders.

Sailors and carpenters had been summoned from Villa Rica with the equipment from the destroyed fleet. They began building 13 brigantines that would be disassembled, hauled in pieces overland, and reassembled on the lake. Cortés was leaving nothing to chance.

The old luck was returning. Two ships put in from Cuba, unaware of the turn of events, bringing arms, powder and equipment for Narváez. Cortés requisitioned them, and appropriated the men and equipment from two ships sent from Jamaica to reprovision Governor Garay's ill-fated ventures. He sent four ships to Hispaniola to bring horses and men. Having determined that swordsmanship alone was not enough, he procured horses, firearms, crossbows, and powder from Española. Finally, the bribe sent to the king in the earliest days of the expedition began to pay off, as arms, equipment, and men began arriving from Spain itself.

As he prepared for the advance, Cortés promulgated a series of orders: no one should blaspheme Christ, the Virgin Mary, the Apostles, or the Saints; no soldier should mistreat or rob the Indian auxiliaries; no soldier should depart from camp for any reason; all

Mexican warriors defending the Great Temple. One may have captured a Spanish standard. From the *Codex Azcatitlan*, plate 24. (Ann Ronan Picture Library/Heritage-Images)

The siege of Tenochtitlán, AD 1521

After two years of failed negotiations, war, and plague, the Aztecs had elected a new emperor, Cuauhtémoc, and began to fortify Tenochtitlán in preparation for a siege by 50,000 troops from Tlaxcala, Huexotzinco, Cholula, among other city states, together with their Spanish allies. The enemy attacked the city by both land and water. But once they had broken into the city, they quickly found themselves trapped within the labyrinth of city streets and canals. Many were lured into dead ends where they were easily crushed to death by stones and rubble cast down by troops positioned on the roofs of buildings. Those who sought to hide or pillage became lost in the mazes of small rooms and patios of private dwellings. Here an Aztec strike force has simultaneously broken through the timber roof and plaster walls of an apartment complex to mercilessly entrap and hack a Tlaxcaltecan and his Spanish ally to pieces. The Spaniard is a captain and master swordsman. The Tlaxcaltecan wears the red and white head band of a nobleman and holds equal rank. His steel sword is a prized gift from the Spaniard. While bowmen pin the enemy down from above, two Aztec warriors have succeeded in breaking through the adobe brick walls of the room to surprise and corner the enemy. One is a nobleman identifiable by his *ehuatl* or tunic. The other is a warrior dressed in a *tlahuiztli* and helmet representing a legendary flaming coyote. Such strategic use of the urban setting forced Cortés to first retreat and then to initiate the siege all over again only by dismantling Tenochtitlán house by house in what would become the longest continuous battle in history. (Adam Hook © Osprey Publishing Ltd)

soldiers should wear good armor (the native armor that many had adopted was to be well quilted), and should wear a neck guard, helmet, and leggings, and carry a shield; no soldier should gamble over a horse or arms; unless sick or wounded, all soldiers were to sleep fully armed and shod, and ready for battle, in case of night attack; sleeping on guard duty, or leaving a post was punishable by death; going from one camp to another without permission was punishable by death; desertion in battle was punishable by death.

Meanwhile, the city of Tenochtitlán was suffering a different scourge. Smallpox had worked its way over the mountains and entered the valley through Chalco, devastating the capital for 60 days. In the Basin of Mexico alone over 40 percent of the farming population succumbed and famine soon followed. Among the dead was the Emperor Cuitláhuac, who was succeeded by a cousin, Cuauhtémoc. Although only 25, his resistance in the final days of the empire would elevate him in the Aztec mind to the greatest of all the emperors and, in modern times, as a symbol of nationalism and independence.

The siege of Mexico, 1521

On December 26, 1520 Cortés marched out of Segura de la Frontera. Besides the well-equipped, reinforced European contingent, he had 10,000 Tlaxcaltecan auxiliaries, and the leaders of Tlaxcala promised more as needed. They crossed the mountains and entered Texcoco unopposed, where they established quarters, and smashed the idols in the temples. Expeditionary forces were sent to the surrounding towns, and many surrendered. Representatives of other towns said they would surrender except for the Mexican garrisons. Occasionally, they would skirmish with Mexican troops. After one particularly fierce fight, Xochimilco fell, and once again Cortés stood on the shores of the lake with the city of Tenochtitlán visible in the distance.

To avoid a protracted siege, Cortés sent peace overtures to Cuauhtémoc. When these were refused, he subjugated the towns around the lake to secure the mainland for a blockade. A company under Gonzalo de Sandoval captured a dependency of Texcoco where they found the flayed faces of two Spaniards, captured during *La Noche Triste* and sacrificed in the temple. The skin was tanned with the beards intact. Other offerings included four horsehides, complete with hooves and shoes, and the clothing of the Spaniards who had been sacrificed. In one of the cages where the victims were held while they waited the knife, a member of the Narváez expedition, Juan Yuste, had scratched his name.

On April 28, the brigantines were launched on Lake Texcoco. Messengers were sent to Tlaxcala, Cholula, Huexotzingo, and other allied states, and within a week the auxiliaries began arriving in Texcoco. Fifty thousand came from Tlaxcala alone, parading into the city with their battle standards, and shouting, "Castile! Castile! Tlaxcala! Tlaxcala!" With the city of Mexico blockaded, Cortés finalized his plans. Alvarado would lead 30 cavalrymen, 18 crossbowmen, 150 infantry, and 25,000 Tlaxcalteca from Tacuba. Olíd would attack from Coyoacán with 33 cavalry, 18 crossbowmen, 160 infantry, and 20,000 native auxiliaries. Sandoval would lead 24 cavalrymen, four musketeers, 13 crossbowmen, 150 infantry, and 30,000 auxiliaries from Itzapalapa. Cortés himself would command the fleet, with each ship carrying a captain, six crossbowmen or musketeers, and 12 oarsmen. The aqueduct carrying fresh water from Chapultepec was cut, and the city was now isolated.

Cortés and his captains began an inspection of the causeways. They ordered some broken sections to be filled so that cavalry might pass, but ahead they saw more breaks and barricades.

On May 31, 1521 Sandoval started out for Itzapalapa to secure the causeway and begin attacking the city. Cortés boarded one of the brigantines and began moving to support Sandoval from the lake. After securing a fortified hill that commanded the water, he turned the ships toward Mexico, where he encountered about 500 canoes loaded with warriors. A fresh breeze blew in from the mainland, the sails filled, and the Spanish fleet smashed through the canoes, wrecking many and drowning the warriors, and driving the rest back to the city. The siege of Mexico had begun.

The next 80 days were desperate. The Spanish fought their way yard by yard along the causeways, only to be pushed back and forced to retake the same ground. On the Tacuba causeway, the site of which is now covered by a broad avenue called Puente de Alvarado (Alvarado's Bridge), Alvarado rashly made a dash to capture the temple precincts. The Aztecs retreated, leaving behind a gap in the causeway of about 60 feet. Alvarado and the cavalry rode into the water and came up on the other side of the break, while the infantry began filling in the gap. Suddenly, canoes swarmed into it, closing a carefully prepared ambush. The brigantines rushed to help, but were wedged up against a barrier of stakes driven into the lake bed just below the surface. Alvarado managed to fight his way back, but five men had been taken alive.

Capture meant sacrifice. Often in the distance, the Spaniards heard the mournful sound of the great temple drum, the conch shell trumpets, and other horns signifying the brutal sacrifice of their comrades. As they pushed farther into the city, and closer to the temple, they could actually see the ceremony on the great platform atop the pyramid, but could do nothing but pray. The soldiers adopted the habit of closing each day of battle with the prayer, "Oh, thanks be to God that they did not carry me off today for sacrifice." As more and more of their companions were dragged to the stones and slaughtered, their hatred of the Aztecs increased. Just as no quarter was expected, none was given.

In battle the Aztecs tried to demoralize the Tlaxcalteca and other auxiliaries by throwing the stewed limbs of sacrificial victims into their ranks, shouting, "Eat the flesh of these *tueles* [gods – a reference to the near divine status in which the Castilians were first held] and of your brothers, because we are sated with it..."

Cortés now ordered a temporary halt, sending small details into the city to maintain the semblance of an offensive. His men had been fighting almost constantly for ten weeks, and the allied states were becoming unnerved at the Aztec tenacity. The uneasiness increased as couriers from Tenochtitlán slipped through the blockade and displayed European body parts as trophies of battle and sacrifice. Spanish troops had to

Many Spanish captives were taken in the summer of 1521. The *Florentine Codex* indicates that they were ritually executed before the great temple of the Aztec god Huitzilopochtli. Even the heads of their horses were displayed as war trophies on the *tzompantli*. (*Florentine Codex* Bk 12, Ch. 35, American Museum of Natural History)

be detached from the main body, and sent around to the allied cities to suitably impress their leaders and keep them in line. The point was made, and when Cortés renewed the offensive in late July, he had 150,000 Indian troops. He now began a policy of devastation. As each block of the city was secured, he demolished the buildings and used them to fill the canals and gaps in the causeways to provide a level field for his soldiers and horses. To make matters worse for the Aztecs, the people of Xochimilco, Cuitláhuac, and Itzapalapa now were making raids of their own, crossing the lake in canoes, plundering and carrying off women and children. Although Cuauhtémoc managed to stop it, the division of his forces between these pirate raids and the Spanish assault seriously hampered his defense.

The city itself was a shambles, and the people were suffering. Already weakened by the recent smallpox epidemic, and with food and water cut off by the blockade, they were dying in great numbers. Many noncombatants were coming to the Spanish lines to give themselves up. Alonso de Aguilar wrote,

> [T]here was a great pestilence in the city because there were so many people there, especially women, and they had nothing more to eat. We soldiers could scarcely get about the streets because of the Indians who were sick from hunger, pestilence and smallpox.

Whatever the atrocities for which the Spaniards may be blamed in the five centuries since the Conquest, their acts paled in comparison to those of their Tlaxcaltecan allies.

ve qʒque q̃uhxacatl.

Centuries of hate and the basic viciousness of Mesoamerican warfare combined in a violence that appalled even Cortés himself. As he later wrote to the king:

> [W]e had more trouble in preventing our allies from killing with such cruelty than we had in fighting the enemy. For no race, however savage, has ever practiced such fierce and unnatural cruelty as the natives of these parts. Our allies also took many spoils that day, which we were unable to prevent, as they numbered more than 150,000 and we Spaniards were only some nine hundred. Neither our precautions nor our warnings could stop their looting, though we did all we could...

The new assault on Tenochtitlán started in December 1520. Throughout the following spring, the Aztecs fought from behind barricades, from roof tops, and canoes in the narrow canals, continually trapping the Spaniards and inflicting devastating casualties. The siege became a war of attrition. (*Lienzo de Tlaxcala*, American Museum of Natural History)

Last Stand at the Great Temple, 1521

During the constant skirmishing throughout the summer of 1521, the Spaniards would succeed in making incursions into the center of Tenochtitlán by day only to be driven back out at nightfall. The city itself became a most ingenious form of defense. The streets of Tenochtitlán were maze-like. Once inside, the Spaniards were unable to penetrate without knowing a specific route and they were easily trapped and attacked from all sides and above. The sacred precinct was walled and the temple pyramids contained within them could be manned as refuges or citadels. The Great Temple rose to over 100 feet in height. It had

steep sides, staircases, and stepped platforms along which troops could arrange themselves to shower weapons and rocks down on the intruders until such time as they could be relieved from other parts of the city. Here an elite Aztec squadron has gathered in the main plaza to make a defensive stand. A Spanish artillery crew, composed of sailors, are directed to fire their lombard on an assault group charging towards them. Nearby is the giant *tzompantli* where the thousands of heads of sacrificial victims from previous Aztec conquests have been displayed. (Adam Hook © Osprey Publishing Ltd)

I had posted Spaniards in every street, so that when the people began to come out [to surrender] they might prevent our allies from killing those wretched people, whose number was uncountable. I also told the captains of our allies that on no account should any of those people be slain; but there were so many that we could not prevent more than fifteen thousand being killed and sacrificed [by the Tlaxcalteca] that day.

By August the resistance had been pushed into a single corner of Tlatelolco. The brigantines began moving into the canals, their gunners firing into the houses. Realizing the situation was hopeless, Cuauhtémoc loaded his family and retainers into canoes and attempted to escape to the mainland. The lake was covered with canoes as people fled the city. When Cortés realized what had happened he ordered the brigantines out into the lake to find the emperor. On August 13, 1521, García Holguín, the captain of a brigantine, recognized the imperial awnings, overtook the canoe, and forced it to surrender. Taken before Cortés, Cuauhtémoc said,

Cuauhtémoc, the last Aztec emperor of Mexico, on a 20th-century Mexican five peso coin. (Collection of Charles M. Robinson)

Lord Malinche, I have kept my obligation in the defense of my city and vassals, and I can do no more, and I am brought by force and impressment into your presence and power. Take that dagger in your belt and kill me.

Cortés responded graciously, praising the beleaguered emperor for his valiant defense. Although he regretted the destruction of the city and the deaths of so many people, he said it was now passed and could not be changed. As for Cuauhtémoc and his followers, their lives would be spared.

The great siege was over. With the conquest of Mexico, one age in the history of the world ended, and a new one was beginning. In the simple, but soaring words of Bernal Díaz del Castillo, "Cuauhtémoc and his captains were apprehended on the thirteenth of August, at the hour of vespers, on the day of the Honorable St. Hipolite, in the year of one thousand five hundred twenty-one. Thanks to Our Lord Jesus Christ, and to Our Lady, the Holy Virgin Mary, His blessed mother. Amen."

AFTER THE VICTORY

Once the Spaniards had conquered the Aztec capital, their immediate thoughts were centered on spoils of war. For three years they had fought and suffered against incredible odds. They had seen their comrades dragged to the temples for sacrifice, and had been powerless to intervene. They had recovered identifiable body parts which had been offered to the pagan gods. Now it was time for payment. The day of the surrender, they raged through the city looking for gold. Meanwhile, their Tlaxcaltecan allies continued their hideous orgy of blood, slaughtering any Aztec they found. The city itself was completely ruined. About 100,000 men, women, and children had died during the 80-day siege, and thousands of corpses lay unburied. Most of the remaining population streamed out along the causeways where the Spaniards set up checkpoints to search for concealed treasure. Noblewomen covered themselves with mud and dressed in rags to hide their status, but the rapacious Spaniards subjected them all to body searches.

Once a substantial amount of gold was collected, it was taken to Cortés's headquarters in Coyoacán, where he and the Crown auditors agreed to have it melted down and assayed. The total came to more than 130,000 *castellanos* (a *castellano* was 42.29g of pure silver). This and all other plunder, including slaves, was tabulated. One-fifth of the total was allocated to the Crown in accordance with the law. The balance was distributed to the army according to rank, with Cortés and his captains naturally getting the lion's share. Additionally, there was a substantial amount of gold ornaments, featherwork, and other objects that the sophisticated Cortés recognized as art. Rather than being parceled out as plunder, these were sent *in toto* to the less than appreciative king-emperor, who had the gold melted down. Some of the featherwork eventually ended up in Vienna, where, if one searches diligently enough, one may see it in the Künsthistorische Museum.

OPPOSITE
Cortés returned to Spain with an entourage that included 40 Indians. Three of Motecuhzoma's sons made the journey, together with a group of acrobats, whose ability to twirl heavy objects with their feet truly amazed the Europeans. (Weidtiz, 1927)

The *Florentine Codex* illustrates
the final defeat of Tenochtitlán,
which was accomplished
through a series of coordinated
amphibious and land-based
attacks. The 13 brigantines
ranged between 42ft and 48ft
in length, and generally only
had one or two sails. They were
flat-bottomed which allowed
them to get in close to secure
the causeways. (*Florentine Codex*,
Bk 12, Ch. 30, American
Museum of Natural History)

The amount of plunder proved disappointing. The great treasure found in the palace
and then lost on *La Noche Triste* was gone. As previously noted, the men had served on
their own account, and now that the war was over, their accumulated debts had to be paid.
Some were so substantial that arbitrators were called in to determine just amounts, and
those without the money to pay were given a two-year grace period. With the constant fear
and stress of the war behind them, the soldiers began to consider their positions and, for
the first time, began to mutter against their commander, believing he had amassed a great
personal fortune at their expense. The royal auditors, likewise, accused him of withholding
treasure that rightfully belonged to the Crown. They little realized that they were dealing
not only with the losses of war, but with the highly developed private enterprise system of
Aztec Mexico; much of the wealth they had seen throughout the city on their arrival two
years earlier belonged not to the state, but to the city's powerful merchant class. These
merchants, naturally, had fled with all they could carry.

His back to the wall, Cortés summoned Cuauhtémoc and the other lords to explain
the loss. They argued among themselves, but could add little. The royal auditor, Julián

Aldrete, demanded that Cuauhtémoc and Tetlepanquetzal, the king of Tacuba, be tortured. Cortés assented, probably with fewer qualms than he later pretended. Their feet were dipped in oil and set ablaze. Finally, Cuauhtémoc said the treasure had been thrown into the lake, but Spanish divers found little that was substantial. Ultimately, this brutality, which left both men permanently lamed, yielded only an additional 200,000 pesos. Once the Crown, the royal bureaucrats, Cortés, and the captains got their shares, the average soldier may have had about 160 pesos for three years of suffering. To put this in perspective, a reasonable sword cost about 50 pesos at the time.

Although large regions of Mesoamerica remained to be subdued, the Conquest was essentially completed with the surrender of Cuauhtémoc. The destruction of the greatest power on the continent had a profound effect on the surrounding states. The only other power capable of serious and prolonged opposition was the Tarascan empire, to the northwest in Michoacán. When word of the Aztec surrender reached the Tarascans, they sent emissaries to Cortés asking to be accepted as vassals. "I replied that we were, in truth, all Your Majesty's vassals," he reported to Charles V, "and that their lord had been

The *Lienzo de Tlaxcala* portrays the baptism of the Tlaxcaltec lords. Cortés spoke ceaselessly about Christianity and even convinced the Tlaxcalteca to remove the idols from one of their temples and replace them with images of the cross and the Virgin Mary. For the Spaniards, the baptism became a very public demonstration of reciprocity in their alliance with the Tlaxcalteca. (*Lienzo de Tlaxcala*, American Museum of Natural History)

wise in wishing to become one also, for we were obliged to make war on those who did not."

Nevertheless, he sent several expeditions to Michoacán, culminating with a reasonably large force (considering the resources) under Cristóbal de Olíd in the summer of 1522. As an example, Olíd plundered the region, throwing down the temples, and sent the Tarascan monarch to Mexico. There, Cortés received him with the full dignity of a ruler, and he returned to Michoacán duly impressed and subdued. Olíd, meanwhile, moved farther north to Colima, which he quickly pacified. Elsewhere, expeditions reached the Pacific. Cortés himself led an expedition to subdue the Pánuco region, in order to head off another colonization attempt by Governor Garay. In one of the towns, they found the flayed facial skin of Castilians from Garay's first expedition. Nevertheless, the Pánuco was subjugated, adding a great agricultural region to the growing empire.

The most remarkable aspect of these expeditions was the number of native auxiliaries under their own chieftains and lords, many of whom had recently been enemies. Besides Tlaxcalteca, they included Texcocans, and even some 15,000 Mexicans provided by Cuauhtémoc and commanded by one of his cousins. The reason for the turnabout was really quite simple: their religion had long foretold the destruction of their world, and now it had come to pass. There was nothing further to do but to assist those who had overthrown that world. Thus, with the help of the defeated Aztecs, virtually all of what is now Mexico came firmly under Spanish rule within a decade or so. Such resistance as did occur came largely from some Maya-controlled areas of Yucatán, which managed to hold out for another century, and in some coastal and desert areas of the far north, to which the Spaniards did not attach any immediate importance. As Cortés noted in his third letter to Charles V, written only nine months after Cuauhtémoc's surrender, "Your Majesty's farms and estates have been established in the cities and provinces which seem the best and most suitable."

Interestingly enough, Cortés also worried about the fate of the Indians. Although he was the instrument of its destruction, he admired much of their civilization, and believed them capable of going about their business unmolested by their new rulers. He was growing particularly uneasy at the thought of enslaving them. Discussing the problem in one of his letters to the emperor, he contended they were of too high a caliber to be relegated to slavery and oppressed to destruction, as was happening in the West Indies. Realistically, however, if they were not enslaved, who would work the estates that the Conquistadores were establishing? Additionally, entire regions had served as allies during the war and, far from being enslaved, their leaders expected to share in the spoils. To avoid outright slavery, yet maintain the economy, he recommended the establishment of an *encomienda*, a system already existing in the West Indies, by which a conquistador or settler would be granted a fixed amount of labor from the Indians living on a specified area of land. The *encomendero*, as the grantee was called, was expected to serve as a guardian of the Indians, to Christianize them, and have them ready for military service if called upon. Cortés required that every *encomendero* plant agricultural produce, which led to the introduction of European food crops into New Spain.

In practice it was much easier for the *encomendero* to require the payment of produce comparable to the specified labor, rather than to go out and attempt to keep a tally on who was working where and when. Consequently the system developed into a tribute, not radically different from that maintained by the Aztecs before the Conquest. With the *encomendero* essentially assuming the role previously held by the native princes, it required little serious adjustment. Although technically the *encomienda* was abolished under the New Laws and other royal edicts, in reality it remained in one form or another, establishing a serfdom that lasted well into the 19th century; some contend that in parts of Mexico it continues.

As more of the country fell to the Spaniards, Cortés realized it needed an administrative center. Although the ruined and pestilential city of Mexico had been abandoned after the surrender, he realized the psychological hold it had over the country. Perhaps, also, he did not want the ruins to become a place of pilgrimage for the defeated peoples, and a possible inspiration for rebellion. In late 1521, he decided to rebuild the city. Town lots were distributed to all who wanted them, and the city was divided into districts governed by various officials according to Spanish custom. While the reconstruction took place, the future population continued to reside in Coyoacán. Nevertheless, by May 1522, he was able to write to the king,

> In the four or five months that we have been rebuilding the city it is already most beautiful… each day it grows more noble, so that just as before it was the capital and center of all these provinces so it shall be henceforth. And it is being so built that the Spaniards will be strong and secure and well in charge of the natives, who will be unable to harm them in any way.

Initially, the job of rebuilding fell to Alvarado. The native auxiliaries, now more a hindrance than an asset, were given ample share of the plunder, and their leaders reconfirmed as lords of the provinces under the new order. Those not necessary to cleaning and rebuilding the city were sent home. Alvarado's tenure as supervisor of reconstruction was shortlived. Early in 1522 he was given the task of subduing Oaxaca, where he remained over a year, collecting substantial treasure. He was en route back to Mexico when he received word from Cortés that the treasure was to be forwarded on to the capital to replace that captured by the French corsairs of Francis I. Alvarado's men, who had imagined themselves wealthy from the plunder, were outraged, and several hatched a plot to murder him and his brothers. Getting wind of it, he arrested the plotters. Two ringleaders were hanged, and the local chief, also part of the conspiracy, was imprisoned, where he died two weeks later. This plot was an early indication of the growing discontent that would plague Cortés and his captains as the Conquest drew to a close.

CONCLUSION

NEW SPAIN
AND NEW LEGACIES

If Balboa's expedition to Panama was the first European toehold on the mainland of the western hemisphere, the Conquest of Mexico was the first squeeze of a vise-like grip that kept more than half of the New World in Spanish hands for some three centuries. As with Columbus before him, the full import of Cortés's achievement was not understood for several decades. Yet Columbus, with his discovery of a continent previously unknown in Europe, and Cortés, with the conquest of a powerful and equally unknown empire, had proven that the unimaginable was possible. They set the stage for the expeditions of Francisco Pizarro and others in South America, and for Francisco Vásquez de Coronado and Hernando de Soto in what is now the United States. In view of the accomplishments of Columbus and Cortés, the search for El Dorado, or for seven golden cities, made perfect sense.

Meanwhile, Mexico became the centerpiece of a vast viceregency designated "New Spain" that extended from the modern American states of Utah and California, south to the Costa Rica–Panama border, and from Puerto Rico in the east across half the world to the Philippines. The administrative seat was the city of Mexico, which rose like a phoenix from the ashes of the Aztec capital of Tenochtitlán. New Spain was the first of a series of viceregencies that extended southward across the hemisphere as Spanish power itself expanded. Next came Peru, which administered western South America; New Granada, northern South America; and finally La Plata, southeastern South America. Only Brazil, firmly in the hands of Portugal, escaped Spanish rule.

It is questionable whether any man besides Cortés could have conquered Mexico. Some argue that if he had not, someone else would have. But as Hugh Thomas notes in his magnificent history of the Conquest, this is total conjecture and cannot be established. The questions must then be raised: would any European besides Cortés have grasped and exploited the differences between the various Indian people? Given the record of most of his contemporaries, who tended to regard all Indians as beneath contempt, it is highly

OPPOSITE
Modern Mexico City.
(Topfoto/The Image Works)

ABOVE
Anton burning Indian nobles, from the *Codex Kingsborough*.
(John Pohl)

An illustration showing the irony of victory for Cortés's Indian allies; Franciscan friars burning the war banners and trophies of the Tlaxcalteca, as well as their sacred idols. (Glasgow University Library)

unlikely, and these political and tribal differences were essential to a Spanish victory. Could any other leader have been so profoundly lucky, and then be blessed with the good sense to realize it? Could any other leader have kept such an absolute hold over an army that was largely composed of unruly adventurers? Not until the city of Tenochtitlán had actually fallen, and the Aztec Empire was relegated to history did Cortés's own men seriously question his leadership. One must particularly admire his ability to maintain the loyalty of his Indian allies in the critical period before the final advance, when *La Noche Triste* had demonstrated how truly vulnerable the Spaniards were.

What would have happened had the Conquest failed? Again, Thomas makes a good case that possibly Spain would have had second thoughts before another attempt at conquest, and that Mexico, like Japan, might then have gone its own way, remaining culturally isolated only to reemerge into European consciousness in a later era.

This, however, is speculation. As Cortés worked with the real problems of consolidating the newly won empire and rebuilding its capital, an entirely new complication arose. His wife, Doña Catalina, arrived uninvited and unexpected from Cuba, bringing with her a retinue suitable for her presumed position as the new vicereine. At the time, Cortés had several mistresses, Indian and Spanish, and was preparing for the birth of his son by Doña Marina. The pair argued and that, combined with the 7,500-foot altitude of Mexico City, no doubt aggravated Doña Catalina's already weak heart. She died under mysterious circumstances, and he was accused of murdering her. Most likely, however, they argued, and this brought on a fatal heart attack.

Equally suspicious was the death of Francisco de Garay, who was brought back to Mexico after his failed second expedition to Pánuco. After dining with Cortés on Christmas Day, 1523, Garay died of an unspecified stomach complaint.

By now, the old restlessness was setting in. Cortés had dispatched Cristóbal de Olíd to Honduras, and in 1524 received word that Olíd had rebelled. Using this as a pretext (and unaware that Olíd had already been defeated and executed by Cortés's supporters), he set off with several thousand Spaniards and native auxiliaries, and all the retinue of a court; he even took in tow the nominal emperor Cuauhtémoc. The expedition was a fiasco, beset by starvation, disease, and rumors of mutiny. When it returned to Mexico two years later, there were fewer than 100 survivors. Cuauhtémoc was not among them; exhausted, paranoid, and suspecting the emperor was conspiring against him, Cortés ordered him hanged.

The remainder of Cortés's life was anticlimactic. He and all the others who had fought so hard, and with such high hopes of fame, wealth, and glory, found themselves displaced by paper-shuffling bureaucrats sent by Charles V to administer the newly conquered kingdom. The rest of Cortés's life was divided between his estates in Mexico and in presenting his case to the king-emperor. He was named Marqués del Valle de Oaxaca, confirmed as captain-general, and given large estates, but he was denied the right to rule his conquests. That would be left to the civil servants, and in the early years, Mexico was governed by some remarkably good ones. Nevertheless, whispering campaigns, prompted largely by envy, prevented Cortés from receiving his full due, and in the end he was treated shabbily. He died on December 2, 1547, bitter, broken, and forgotten. His body was later returned to Mexico City, where it was buried in the Hospital of Jesus, which he had founded at the height of his power and prestige.

The fiery Pedro de Alvarado used the Conquest as the stepping stone to his own career as explorer and conqueror. Subjugating Guatemala, he was appointed governor of that province and of Honduras, but, as restless as his old commander, he could not resist new adventures. In 1541 he was assisting the acting governor of Jalisco, Cristóbal de Oñate, in besieging a native town. He was on foot in full armor when a horse slipped and fell on him. Crushed under the weight of horse and armor, he died about an hour later. Even in death, he was not safe from the bureaucrats, and within a year, his widow had lost many of his estates to the Crown.

In 1526, another of Cortés's officers, Francisco de Montejo, received permission to invade the Yucatán Peninsula. Friars accompanying the expedition wrote of unspeakable cruelties that were inflicted on the Maya people and yet they continued to fight for more

The *Codex Kingsborough* graphically depicts the horrors that were inflicted on the Aztec Indian people through the *encomienda* system. Here Cortés's agent Anton burns four Indian nobles to death. (Ancient Art and Architecture)

than 20 long years. Montejo would later attribute some of his difficulties to Gonzalo Guerrero, a former Spanish soldier who had miraculously survived shipwreck and captivity to become a mighty Maya warlord.

In 1529, Nuño de Guzmán, an ally of Velásquez against Cortés, found himself in a compromising political situation and hoped to win royal favor with an attack on the kingdoms of West Mexico. Invading with an allied army of thousands of Indian and Spanish troops, he cut a bloody swath from Michoacán to Sonora. In one brutal incident he had the king of the Purépecha nearly dragged to death behind a horse before burning him alive. Scores of villages were then put to the torch and thousands of people were enslaved.

Shortly thereafter, reports of cities of gold began to come in from the northern frontier. Indeed, the shipwrecked second-in-command of Narváez's lost expedition, Cabeza de Vaca, walked out of the desert in 1537 to confirm the existence of Indian peoples living in large communities. Eager to capitalize on Nuño's successes, a new expedition was formulated under Francisco Vásquez de Coronado. In 1540, over 300 Spanish troops, hundreds of Indian mercenaries, and a thousand horses and swine marched into what is today Arizona and New Mexico only to find the Pueblo peoples living in cities of adobe. While the troops were away, the Indians of West Mexico rose up in open revolt and attacked isolated Spanish ranches. When the regional governor

The battle of Cajamarca, 1532

Since the days of Columbus, horses had played a fundamental role in all Conquistador expeditions. Indian people generally regarded them as mythical in nature often comparing them to giant deer until they learned their weaknesses. The Aztecs eventually learned to use pikes against them but only very late when the war had already been lost. Learning of Atahualpa's arrival at Cajamarca, Pizarro set a trap for the Inca emperor. First a friar read the *requerimiento*, a "required" document that outlined the Spaniards' divine rights of conquest. Dismissing it, Atahualpa pointed to the sun and remarked that his own god lived in the heavens, where he looked down upon his own children. In that instant, matchlocks blasted from the doorways where the Spaniards had concealed themselves and with shouts of "Santiago! Y a ellos!" ("Saint James and at them!") the cavalry, led by Hernando de Soto, charged directly at Atahualpa's bodyguard with devastating effect. Hooves rang across the courtyard and then thudded against the bare flesh of bodies too tightly packed to flee. Swords rended limbs and lances cut straight through two men at a time. The Inca army was totally surprised and overwhelmed by their first encounter with the horse in warfare. Pizarro himself then charged on foot, cutting his way with sword and dagger to Atahualpa to seize the emperor as his hostage. (Adam Hook © Osprey Publishing Ltd)

failed to subdue the insurgents, Pedro de Alvarado's aid was enlisted, but the "Great Mixtón War," as it came to be known, was only concluded when the viceroy himself took the field with fresh troops.

Events in South America would turn out very differently for the Conquistador Francisco Pizarro. Pizarro had campaigned with Vasco Nuñez de Balboa in 1513 and later became a prominent citizen and landowner in what is today Panama. Restless in middle age, Pizarro embarked on two expeditions south along the coast of Colombia and Ecuador where he bartered for Inca gold. He won the emperor's permission to organize a third expedition to advance into Peru in 1532. Here the Inca controlled an empire of over 700,000 square miles, occupied by ten million people. Learning that Emperor

Today in Mexico, vestiges of Aztec might are everywhere. The modern city of Mexico, built directly on top of the Aztec capital, is a treasure house of the pre-Conquest. Virtually any public works project uncovers some aspect of the original city. The construction of the great metro system in the late 1960s and early 1970s, and even something as mundane as sewer line repairs, have led to important new discoveries. Perhaps the most poignant site in modern Mexico City is Tlatelolco, excavated in the early 1960s to become part of a government showpiece known as the "Plaza of the Three Cultures." Immediately south of the broad avenue of San Juan de Letrán is the great temple compound, including the base of the 114 steps described by Bernal Díaz. Indeed, his narrative is so complete that, using his book as a guide, the visitor can still identify many of the ruins. This represents the ancient culture. Immediately behind is the college-convent of Santa Cruz de Tlatelolco, founded in 1536 by Bishop Zumárraga, and representing the colonial culture. Beyond that, devastated by the great earthquake and subsequently rebuilt, are the steel and glass high-rises of the modern culture. To the rear of the temple complex is a stele with the inscription: "On August 13, 1521, after a heroic defense by Cuauhtémoc, Tlatelolco fell to the power of Hernán Cortés. This was neither a triumph nor a defeat, but rather the painful birth of the Mestizo nation that is the Mexico of today." (Topfoto/The Image Works)

Atahualpa was camped at Cajamarca, Pizarro boldly attacked the Inca army and seized the ruler holding him hostage until he promised to fill a room with gold and other valuables for his ransom. Incredibly, the treasure yielded 13,400lb of gold and 26,000lb of silver. Pizarro then had Atahualpa garroted. After a series of skirmishes, the Spaniards captured the Inca capital of Cuzco itself in 1533. Resistance continued until the 1570s but the ultimate outcome was inevitable.

Enriched by his share in Atahualpa's ransom, Pizarro's cavalry commander, Hernando de Soto, personally financed an invasion of Florida in 1539 despite the dismal failure of two previous expeditions under de León and Narváez. Over the next three years, the army wandered almost aimlessly through Georgia, the Carolinas, Tennessee, Alabama, Mississippi, Louisiana, Arkansas, and Texas before fleeing for their lives down the Mississippi River with a confederated Indian army in hot pursuit. Despite acquiring some 50lb of freshwater pearls, the expedition was a financial disaster that cost de Soto his life.

In the end, it might be argued that some of the ordinary soldiers, like crusty old Bernal Díaz reminiscing on his Guatemalan estates, gained the most. They, after all, had learned to expect the least. Díaz complained of poverty, but poverty is relative. Compared to what might have been, he was, indeed, poor. But by the standards of his era or ours, he ended his days a wealthy man.

The Conquest inaugurated a bitter history of foreign intervention in Mexico. After Spain came military invasions by the United States and France, followed by the economic colonialism of Great Britain, the Netherlands, Germany, and, once again, the United States. This has left Mexico with a particularly xenophobic nationalism. Although the average Mexican takes a kindly and gracious view of foreigners as individuals, he does not necessarily feel the same toward the nations of which they are citizens.

The uneasiness toward foreigners began toward the end of the colonial period, as the winds of the Enlightenment and the full implications of US independence from Great Britain drifted into Mexico, creating a sense of nationhood. Spain, by then in irreversible decline, could do little to maintain Mexican loyalty. In fact, there had been little during the entire colonial period to inspire allegiance. Although the people of the New World dominions were technically Spanish subjects, and the New World provinces themselves were designated as "kingdoms" rather than colonies, the relationship was one of master and serf, and a foreign master at that. Civil administration was in the hands of *peninsulares*, people born in Spain, or European-born foreigners in Spanish service, for whom Mexico was little more than a career assignment. They were forbidden by law to own estates, livestock, or interest in mines in the areas of their jurisdiction. This law was designed to avoid corruption and conflicts of interest, but on those rare occasions when it was enforced, it only increased the sense of estrangement between ruler and subject.

Below the *peninsulares* were the *creoles*, Spaniards of pure European descent but born in the New World, who made up the landed gentry and the officer corps of the colonial armies, but by and large were prohibited from participating in civic affairs. The third class was the *mestizo*, the mixed bloods, who were mainly small merchants,

artisans, and craftsmen. At the bottom were the native Indians, whose sole purpose was to serve as laborers. Such a caste system effectively stifled any effort at advancement by Mexicans of whatever ancestry, and when the Spanish regime collapsed in 1821, the country was ill-prepared for self-government. The first decades of independence were largely a history of military dictatorships, as the *creole* generals were the only ones with any sort of administrative experience.

Even independence did not completely remove Spain from the scene. For several years afterwards, the Spaniards continued to hold the fortress of San Juan de Ulúa, guarding the entrance to Veracruz, and in 1829 Spain actually made a futile attempt to reoccupy the country, which resulted in its final expulsion. As late as the 1840s, however, Mexican monarchists conspired with Spanish representatives to place a Spanish prince on the now defunct Mexican throne.

This long heritage of ill-feeling has produced a Mexican attitude toward Spain that is, at best, ambiguous. While other nations in Latin America honor the old discoverers and conquerors on coins, monuments, and with street names, and the like, there is scarcely a mention of Cortés. Conversely, Cuauhtémoc is a national hero, and his name

This modern reconstruction shows the precinct of the Great Temple of Tenochtitlán as it appeared in 1519. The temple itself, surmounted by the twin sanctuaries of Huitzilopochtli and Tlaloc is at the rear. Immediately in front is the round platform for gladiatorial sacrifices, and the round temple of Quetzalcoatl. To the right is the great *tzompantli*, the rack displaying the heads of sacrificial victims, and immediately in front, the ball court.

The archaeological recovery of the Great Temple began in earnest in 1978. The site had long been known, and once the decision was made, several blocks of colonial buildings of no particular historical or architectural importance were condemned and leveled, to clear the area for excavation. Today the visitor can walk on elevated ramps through the vast ruin, which includes not only the temple itself, but ceremonial halls. Yet this is only a portion of the complex recorded by Cortés and his men; the remainder lies under colonial structures that are themselves deemed irreplaceable monuments and therefore cannot be removed. (Topfoto/The Image Works)

and presumed likeness appear everywhere. Perhaps the final expression of national indifference was Mexico's refusal to establish diplomatic relations with the Franco regime in Spain.

The chaos of Mexico in the mid-19th century produced one of those ironies that so delight historians. During the French intervention of 1862–67, Napoleon III convinced the Habsburg Archduke Maximilian to accept a Mexican throne. He reigned for three years, struggling against an opposition Republican government led by Benito Juárez, a full-blooded Zapotec Indian. When French support was withdrawn, the empire collapsed, and Maximilian surrendered to the Republicans. More than three centuries earlier, a Castilian adventurer had conquered Indian Mexico on behalf of a Habsburg prince. Now Juárez, the Mexican Indian, ordered the death of a Habsburg prince.

The Spanish imprint on Mexican life and culture is everywhere. Every Mexican city and town that existed prior to the 20th century has its colonial monuments. The churches copy those of Spain, many of which were influenced by or converted from the mosques of Spanish Islam; although many Mexican churches were also influenced by Mesoamerican temple construction techniques and traditions. The houses of the well-to-do, plain and drab on the outside and luxurious inside, can likewise be traced to Muslim Spain. Aside from the Spanish Islamic influence, one also sees majestic Renaissance and Baroque colonial mansions and public buildings. The great city of Guanajuato, a cradle of Mexican independence, is nevertheless entirely European, a center of Spanish culture in the New World, with its modern statues of Don Quixote de la Mancha and the faithful Sancho Panza, and an annual Cervantes festival.

Yet the Spanish influence goes beyond art, literature, and architecture. It permeates the daily lives of the Mexican people. They speak a Mexicanized form of Castilian. They use Napoleonic law, and their social attitudes historically have reflected those of Spain.

Dramatic changes to our perception of the Aztecs have come with the critical reappraisal of Conquest histories in recent years. For centuries, Spanish accounts portrayed the defeat of the Aztec empire as a brilliant military achievement with Cortés's vastly outnumbered but better armed troops defeating hordes of superstitious savages. This view continued throughout the 19th and 20th centuries with the popularity of Prescott's *The History of the Conquest of Mexico*. The fact is that the Spaniards owed their success more to Aztec political factionalism and disease, than superior arms and training. In nearly all their battles, the Spaniards were fighting together with Indian allied armies numbering in the tens of thousands. The Conquest was therefore just as much an Indian civil war as a clash of cultures. Today it is the Aztec civilization that is officially embraced as the national heritage of Mexico while over 25 million people, about 30% of the population, still claim direct Indian ancestry.

The Spanish desire for gold was equaled only by their zeal to impose their own religion. Interestingly enough, Christianity took root with remarkable ease. To the people, the destruction of the Aztec civilization meant their own gods had deserted them, creating a spiritual void. Additionally, the Mexican concept of gods shedding their own blood and the blood offerings in their temples meant that little mental adjustment was required to accept the notion of a god-king offering His blood for the benefit of the world, or the symbolic "drinking of blood" in the Christian Communion. In fact, there were enough parallels that the distinction between native belief and Christianity became blurred, creating a uniquely Mexican form of Catholicism. Ancient rituals are celebrated on Christian holidays, and many of the old gods have been transposed into Christian saints with similar characteristics. Perhaps the most famous is the Virgin of Guadalupe, which tradition states appeared to a humble Indian, Juan Diego, at Tepeyac in 1531.

A detail from the *Florentine Codex*, showing Bernardino de Sahagún (1499–1590), the Spanish missionary who chronicled the languages, customs and habits of the peoples of the New World in minute detail. (*Florentine Codex*, American Museum of Natural History)

Interestingly enough, Tepeyac was sacred to the goddess Tonantzin, who was also viewed as a sort of mother figure.

Ironically, the founders of this new faith were the earliest Spanish friars, who did not study the old beliefs, and therefore did not recognize the continuing practice of ancient ways under the guise of Christianity. The first missionary to realize this was the Franciscan Bernardino de Sahagún (1499–1590), who spent the latter two-thirds of his long life in Mexico, and was the first to apply what we now would call anthropological field work to studying virtually every

Not all of Mexico was "conquered." Many nations were incorporated into the Spanish colonial administration peacefully under the leadership of the indigenous nobility. This scene portrays the Mixtec nobleman Domingo de Guzmán conferring with Vicar Domingo de Santa Maria over a theological issue. The Indian king, or *cacique* as he was called, holds a codex or indigenous book of pictographs in his hands discussing the genealogy of his divine royal ancestors with the friar who holds a bible. Behind them approaches the inquisitive Spanish *encomendero*, Francisco de las Casas. Factional disputes soon emerged over the administration of Indian lands between the Conquistadores, the church, and the Indian nobility. Cortés spent much time in Spain arguing claims to greater titles and more territory, not being satisfied with his appointment as Marqués del Valle de Oaxaca where the Mixtecs and Zapotecs controlled so many rich gold mines.

In Cortés's absence, his son Martín and other relatives were appointed *encomenderos*, which entitled them to extract tribute in free labor. Francisco de las Casas, a cousin, was awarded the *encomienda* of Yanhuitlan (a rich province) but it was not long before he found himself embroiled in disputes with the Dominican friars over the administration of this kingdom. Although Guzmán, also known as Lord Seven Monkey, was a direct descendant of the epic hero Eight Deer, the *encomendero* felt it was his right to rule as a feudal lord and resented the Dominican's involvement with the *cacique*. Acting as an effective mediator between the crown and the indigenous nobility who really controlled the land, the church eventually succeeded in forming the more lucrative partnership. By the 17th century the *encomenderos* and their descendants had become largely disenfranchised and their legacy as Conquistadores was forgotten. (Adam Hook © Osprey Publishing Ltd)

D. Antonius D Mendoça. 1ᵒ. noua Hispanie Pro
Rex et dux Generalis Año. 1535.

Don Antonio de Mendoza (1490–1552), who became viceroy of New Spain in 1535, was the first in a long line of bureaucrats who replaced the original conquerors in administering the new domains. (Museo Nacional de Historia, Mexico)

aspect of pre-Conquest Mexico. Sahagún's monumental *Historia general de las cosas de la Nueva España* ("General History of the Things of New Spain"), more popularly known as the *Florentine Codex*, is a detailed study of virtually every aspect of pre-Conquest life in Mexico, from history, religion, and philosophy, to trade and economics.

There is no question that Sahagún's motivation was to understand Mexican beliefs so that he could combat idolatry. Yet as the work progressed, it almost took on a life of its own. Working through his Mexican students, who had supplemented their own Nahuatl language with Castilian and Latin, Sahagún met with native elders and scholars, studying their pictorial records, and listening to their accounts of their now vanished world. The linguistic aspect fascinated him. Although Nahuatl was devoid of a formal style of writing, the Mexicans nevertheless used pictographs to express an idea. Many of these were reproduced in the *General History* together with the Nahuatl record written in the Roman alphabet, and its Castilian paraphrase and commentary. Sahagún studied Aztec monuments, and found much to admire in their history and culture. The basic work, compiled from about 1558 to 1580, was organized, European style, into 12 books categorized according to subject, with the text divided into chapters and paragraphs. The twelfth book, a history of the Conquest itself from the Aztec persepective, was expanded into a much more extensive account in 1585, based on subsequent research with allowances for changes in Sahagún's own perspectives. When completed, the *General History* was so comprehensive, and the main body so dispassionate, that it must serve as the basis of any modern work on the Aztec civilization.

Another important account of ancient Mexico originated from an equally unlikely source, the Spanish Crown. There exists today in the Bodleian Library in Oxford, an earlier manuscript than either Sahagún or Durán, known as the *Codex Mendoza*. It was compiled in Mexico City about 1541 by native scribes working under friars, at the instigation of Charles V, who wanted to know more about his overseas dominions. Because the imperial commission for the manuscript apparently came from the viceroy, Don Antonio de Mendoza, it carries his name.

The text of the *Codex Mendoza* combines the Mexican pictographs with written explanations in Spanish and Nahuatl. As such, it serves, in the words of one scholar, as "a kind of Rosetta stone." The glyphs and illustrations portray virtually every aspect of Mexican society, including tributary kingdoms, lists of tribute, illustrations of textiles, arms and armor, costumes, foods, and even the thread of daily life for citizens of various classes. As such, it is a comprehensive visual image of the Aztec empire. The inspiration for much of this work came from Juan de Zumárraga, the first Bishop of Mexico, who initially arrived in the country in 1528. Like the early settler Bartolomé de las Casas, Zumárraga saw himself as a protector of the Indians. His methods, however, were far more subtle than those of las Casas. For that reason, plus the fact that he also served as apostolic inquisitor, history often pillories him as a guardian of the conquering status quo. Yet, despite his zeal in protecting and expanding the faith, Zumárraga promoted learning and was open to different ideas. He believed that the Mexicans were capable of acquiring the best of Spanish culture, and also that (religion aside) their own culture contained much that was admirable. The schools that he founded or sponsored paved the way for the Nahua-Spanish scholars who were indispensable to men like Sahagún and Durán. It was Zumárraga, also, who purportedly interviewed Juan Diego concerning his vision of the Virgin of Guadalupe. Although the validity of the apparition, and even the actual existence of Juan Diego has been questioned by both Roman Catholic and non-Roman Catholic scholars, Pope John Paul II nevertheless canonized Juan Diego as a saint of the Church during his Episcopal visit to Mexico in the fall of 2001.

BIBLIOGRAPHY AND FURTHER READING

PRIMARY SOURCES

Berdan, Frances F., and Anawalt, Patricia Rieff (eds.), *The Essential Codex Mendoza* (University of California Press, Berkeley, 1997)

Chavero, Alfredo, *Lienzo de Tlaxcala* (Mexico, 1892)

Columbus, Christopher, *Four Voyages to the New World: letters and selected documents*, trans. and ed. by R. H. Major (Corinth Books, New York, 1961)

Cortés, Hernán, *Letters from Mexico*, trans. and ed. by A. R. Pagden (Grossman Publishers, New York, 1971)

Díaz del Castillo, Bernal, *Historia Verdadera de la Conquista de la Nueva España*, 5th edition (Editorial Porrua, S.A., Mexico, D.F.,1960)

Díaz del Castillo, Bernal, *The Discovery and Conquest of Mexico*, trans. by A. P. Maudsley (Farrar, Straus & Cudahy, New York, 1956)

Durán, Diego (comp.), *The History of the Indies of New Spain*, trans. and annot. by Doris Heyden (University of Oklahoma Press, Norman, 1994)

De Fuentes, Patricia (ed. and trans.), *The Conquistadores: First-Person Accounts of the Conquest of Mexico* (The Orion Press, New York, 1963)

Hassig, Ross, *Mexico and the Spanish Conquest* (Longman, London, 1994)

León-Portilla, Miguel (ed.), *The Broken Spears: The Aztec Account of the Conquest of Mexico* (Constable and Company Ltd., London, 1962)

López de Gómara, Francisco, *Cortés: The Life of the Conqueror by his Secretary*, trans. and ed. by Lesley Byrd Simpson (University of California Press, Berkeley, 1964)

Sahagún, Bernardino de (comp.), *The Conquest of New Spain*, 1585 revision (University of Utah Press, Salt Lake City, 1989)

Sahagún, Bernardino de (comp.), *Florentine Codex: General History of the Things of New Spain*, trans. by Arthur J. O. Anderson and Charles E. Dibble, 12 vols (School of American Research, Santa Fe, 1950–82)

Sahagún, Bernardino de, *Primeros Memoriales*, 2 vols, photography by Ferdinand Anders, paleography of Nahuatl text and English translation by Thelma D. Sullivan, completed and revised with additions by H. B. Nicholson, Arthur J. O. Anderson, Charles E. Dibble, Eloise Quiñones Keber and Wayne Ruwet (University of Oklahoma, Norman, 1993–1997)

Thomas, Hugh, *Conquest: Montezuma, Cortés, and the Fall of Old Mexico* (Simon & Schuster, New York, 1993)

Thomas, Hugh, *Who's Who of the Conquistadores* (Cassell and Co., 2000)

SECONDARY SOURCES

Anawalt, Patricia Rieff, "What Price Aztec Pageantry?" in *Archaeology* Vol. 30/4 (1977), pp. 226–233.

Anawalt, Patricia Rieff, *Indian Clothing Before Cortés: Mesoamerican Costumes from the Codices* (University of Oklahoma Press, Norman, 1981)

Anawalt, Patricia Rieff, "Understanding Aztec Human Sacrifice," in *Archaeology* Vol. 35/5 (1982), pp. 38–45.

Anawalt, Patricia Rieff, "Riddle of the Aztec Royal Robe," in *Archaeology* Vol. 46/3 (1993), pp. 30–36.

Atkinson, William C., *A History of Spain and Portugal* (Penguin Books Ltd., London, 1960)

Bancroft, Hubert Howe, *History of Mexico, Vol. 2*, from *The Works of Hubert Howe Bancroft*, 39 vols (A. L. Bancroft & Co., San Francisco, 1883)

Boone, Elizabeth Hill, *The Aztec World*, in *Exploring the Ancient World* series (St. Remy Press, Montreal, and Smithsonian Institution, Washington DC, 1994)

Boorstin, Daniel, *The Discoverers* (Random House, New York, 1983)

Broda, Johanna, Carrasco, Davíd & Matos Moctezuma, Eduardo, *The Great Temple of Tenochtitlán: Center and periphery in the Aztec World* (University of California Press, Berkeley, 1987)

Brumfiel, Elizabeth M., "Elite and Utilitarian Crafts in the Aztec State," in Elizabeth M. Brumfiel & Timothy K. Earle (eds.), *Specialization, Exchange and Complex Societies* (Cambridge University Press, Cambridge, 1987), pp.102–118.

Carrasco, Davíd and Matos Moctezuma, Eduardo, *Moctezuma's Mexico: Visions of the Aztec World* (University of Colorado Press, Niwot, 1992)

Carrasco, Pedro, *The Tenochca Empire of Ancient Mexico: The Triple Alliance of Tenochtitlán, Tetzcoco, and Tlacopan* (University of Oklahoma Press, Norman, 1999)

Carrasco, Pedro, "Social Organization of Ancient Mexico," in Gordon Elkholm & Ignacio Bernal (eds.), *Handbook of Middle American Indians, Vol. 10* (University of Texas Press, Austin, 1964–76), pp.349–375.

Caso, Alfonso, *The Aztecs, People of the Sun*, 5th edition (University of Oklahoma Press, Norman, 1978)

Cerwin, Herbert, *Bernal Diaz, Historian of the Conquest* (University of Oklahoma Press, Norman, 1963)

Clendinnen, Inga, *Aztecs: An Interpretation* (Cambridge University Press, Cambridge, 1991)

Chimalpahin Quauhtlehuantzin, Domingo de San Antón Muñón, *Codex Chimalpahin: Society and Politics in Mexico Tenochtitlán, Tlatelolco, Texcoco, Culhaucan, and Other Nahua Atlepetl in Central Mexico: The Nahuatl and Spanish Annals and Accounts Collected and Recorded by don Domingo de San Anton Munon Chimalpahin Quauhtlehuantzin*, ed. and trans. by Arthur J. O. Anderson and Susan Schroeder, (University of Oklahoma Press, Norman, 1997)

Cypess, Sandra Messinger, *La Malinche in Mexican Literature From History to Myth* (University of Texas Press, Austin, 1991, reprinted 2000)

Davies, Nigel, *The Aztecs, A History* (University of Oklahoma Press, Norman, 1980)

Fagan, Brian, *The Aztecs* (W. H. Freeman and Co, New York, 1984)

Florescano, Enrique, *El Mito de Quetzalcóatl* (Fondo de Cultura Económica, Mexico 1993)

Gillespie, Susan D., *The Aztec Kings: The Construction of Rulership in Mexica History* (University of Arizona Press, Tucson, 1989)

Gush, George, *Renaissance Armies: 1480–1650* (Patrick Stephens, Cambridge, 1975)

Hassig, Ross, *Aztec Warfare: Imperial Expansion and Political Control* (University of Oklahoma Press, Norman, 1988, reprinted 1995)

Hassig, Ross, *War and Society in Ancient Mesoamerica* (University of California Press, Berkeley, 1992)

Heath, Ian, *The Armies of the Aztec and Inca Empires, Other Native Peoples of the Americas, and the Conquistadores 1450–1608*, from *Armies of the 16th Century* series, Vol 2 (Foundry Books, Nottingham, 1999)

Held, Robert, *The Age of Firearms: A Pictorial History from the Invention of Gunpowder to the Advent of the Modern Breechloader* (The Gun Digest Company, Chicago, 1970)

Hillerbrand, Hans J., "The Reforming Spirit," in Merle Severy (ed.), *Great Religions of the World* (National Geographic Society, Washington, 1971)

Humble, Richard, et al., *The Explorers*, from *The Seafarers* series (Time-Life Books, Alexandria, Virginia, 1978)

Innes, Hammond, *The Conquistadores* (Alfred A. Knopf, New York, 1969)

Kelly, John Eoghan, *Pedro de Alvarado, Conquistador* (Princeton University Press, Princeton, New Jersey, 1932)

Kendall, Paul Murray, "The World of Francis I," in *The Renaissance, Maker of Modern Man* (National Geographic Society, Washington, 1970)

Klein, Cecelia, "The Ideology of Autosacrifice at the Templo Mayor," in Elizabeth H. Boone (ed.), *The Aztec Templo Mayor* (Dumbarton Oaks, Washington DC, 1987) pp. 293–370.

Lavin, James D., *A History of Spanish Firearms* (Herbert Jenkins, London, 1965)

Léon-Portilla, Miguel, *Pre-Columbian Literatures of Mexico* (University of Oklahoma Press, Norman, 1969)

León-Portilla, Miguel, *Bernardino de Sahagún, First Anthropologist*, trans. by Mauricio J. Mixco (University of Oklahoma Press, Norman, 2002)

Livesey, Anthony, *Great Commanders and their Battles* (Macmillan, London, 1987)

Lockhart, James, *The Nahuas after the Conquest: A Social and Cultural History of the Indians of Central Mexico* (Stanford University Press, Stanford, 1992)

López de Gómara, Francisco, *Cortés: The Life of the Conqueror by His Secretary* (University of California Press, Berkeley, 1964)

Matos Moctezuma, Eduardo, *The Great Temple of the Aztecs: Treasures of Tenochtitlán* (Thames and Hudson, London, 1988)

Miller, Hubert J., *Juan de Zumárraga: First Bishop of Mexico* (New Santander Press, Texas, 1973)

Nicholson, H. B., "Religion in Pre-Hispanic Central Mexico," in Gordon Ekholm & Ignacio Bernal (eds), *Handbook of Middle American Indians, Vol. 10* (University of Texas Press, Austin, 1971) pp.395–446.

Nicholson, H. B., *Topiltzin Quetzalcoatl of Tollan: a Problem in Mesoamerican Ethnohistory* (University of Colorado Press, Boulder, 2001)

Nicholson, H.B. with Quiñones Keber, Eloise, *Art of Aztec Mexico: Treasures of Tenochtitlán* (National Gallery of Art, Washington, DC, 1983)

Nicolle, David, *Fornovo 1495*, Campaign 43 (Osprey Publishing, Oxford, 1996)

Nicolle, David, *Pavia 1525*, Campaign 44 (Osprey Publishing, Oxford, 1996)

Nicolle, David, *Granada 1492*, Campaign 53 (Osprey Publishing, Oxford, 1998)

Oman, C. W. C., *The Art of War in the Middle Ages*, rev. and ed. by John H. Beeler (Cornell University Press, Cornell, 1968)

Pasztory, Esther, *Aztec Art* (Harry N. Abrams Inc, New York, 1983)

Pohl, John M. D., *Exploring Mesoamerica* (Oxford University Press, Oxford, 1999)

Peterson, Harold L., *Arms and Armor in Colonial America 1526–1783* (Stackpole Co, Harrisburg, 1956)

Peterson, Harold L., *The Treasury of the Gun* (Ridge Press and Golden Press, 1962)

Prescott, William Hickling, *History of the Conquest of Mexico*, 1843 (Reprinted by the Modern Library, New York, 1998)

Quiñones Keber, Eloise, *Codex Telleriano Remensis* (University of Texas Press, Austin, 1995)

Sauer, Carl Ortwin, *The Early Spanish Main* (University of California Press, Berkeley, 1966)

Smith, Michael E., *The Aztecs* (Blackwell Publishers, Oxford, 1994)

Soustelle, Jacques, *The Daily Life of the Aztecs on the Eve of the Spanish Conquest* (The Macmillan Company, New York, 1962)

Stewart, Desmond, et al., *The Alhambra* (Newsweek, New York, 1974)

Stone, George Cameron, *A Glossary of the Construction, Decoration, and Use of Arms and Armor in all Countries and in all Times Together with Some Closely Related Topics* (Jack Brussel, New York, 1961)

Stuart, Gene S., *The Mighty Aztecs* (The National Geographic Society, Washington DC, 1981)

Time-Life Books (ed.), *Gods of Sun and Sacrifice: Aztec & Maya Myth*, from *Myth and Mankind* series (Time-Life Books BV, Amsterdam, 1997)

Townsend, Richard, *The Aztecs* (Thames and Hudson, London, 1992)

Weiditz, Christoph, *Das Trachtenbuch des Christoph Weiditz von seinen Reisen nach Spanien (1529) und den Niederlanden*, ed. by Theodor Hampfe (Walter de Gruyter & Co., Berlin, 1927)

Wise, Terence, *The Conquistadores*, Men-at-Arms 101 (Osprey Publishing, London, 1980)

Wood, Peter et al, *The Spanish Main*, from *The Seafarers* series (Time-Life Books, Alexandria, Virginia, 1979)

GLOSSARY

adarga a leather, heart-shaped shield

armet the most common late-15th-century horseman's helmet

atlatl ~~Aztec~~ Mexica spear-thrower

Axayacatl (*r.* 1469–81) third Aztec emperor and father of the emperors Motecuhzoma and Cuitláhuac. Cortés was quartered in his palace

NO! **Aztec** "~~People~~ inhabitants of Aztlán" or Place of the ~~Heron, collective name for the Nahuatl-speaking peoples of the Basin of Mexico~~

barbute type of helmet that exposed the face

buffe chin protector worn with a helmet

burgonet open helmet, with a brim projecting over the eyes and a standing comb

Cacama, King of Texcoco (*r.* 1515–20) also called Cacamatzin, distant cousin of Motecuhzoma. His father was the great Texcocoan king and statesman Nezahualpilli (*r.* 1472–1515). Cacama met Cortés en route to Mexico and led him to the city. Died under mysterious circumstances during *La Noche Triste*, probably murdered on Cortés's orders

calmecac Aztec priest's school

Camaxtli name for Mixcoatl, father of Quetzalcoatl of legend

caudillo a Spanish captain

celata a type of Spanish helmet

chapel de fer an open helmet with a low crown and a broad round brim worn from the 12th to the 16th century

chinampa an Aztec artificial island field for planting

Coanacoch (*r.* 1520–21) brother of Cacama, placed on the Texcocoan throne in 1520 after the latter's arrest by Cortés

Coixtlahuaca Mixtec-Chocho kingdom of Oaxaca

cuahchic special Aztec warrior rank

Cualpopoca (*d.* 1520) Mexican governor of the Pánuco and instigator of an uprising against the Spaniards on the coast. Burned at the stake toward the end of 1520

Cuauhtémoc (*c.* 1496–1525) (also called by the Spaniards Guatémoc, Guatemotzin) eighth and last emperor. Reigned 1520–21. Son of Ahuítzotl, fifth emperor (*r.* 1486–1502), and a cousin of Motecuhzoma. Surrendered to Cortés on August 13, 1521. Hanged in 1525, during Cortés's Honduras expedition

cuextecatl special Aztec warrior rank

Cuitláhuac (*d.* 1520) seventh emperor, son of Axayacatl and brother of Motecuhzoma, whom he succeeded after his deposition. Reigned for a few months until his death of smallpox

Doña Marina (*c.* 1502–51) native name Malinalli, malintli ~ malintzin also known as la Malinche. Indian girl given to the Spaniards at Potonchán. Speaking both Chontal Maya and Nahuatl, she became Cortés's interpreter and, to a certain extent, confidante, adviser, and spy. She also bore him a son. Married after the Conquest to Juan Jaramillo, she lived quietly on her estates until her death

doublet close-fitting jacket worn by Spanish men of the 16th century

ehuatl battle tunic worn by Aztec noblemen

hidalgo a rank of minor Spanish nobility

ichcahuipilli Aztec cotton quilted armor

Huaxtec Indian people of northern Veracruz

huey tlatoani literally "great speaker," the Aztec emperor

Huitzilopochtli Hummingbird ~~of the South~~, patron god of the Aztecs

jerkin a type of overcoat or vest worn in a variety of styles either with or without sleeves

macehual Aztec peasant

macuahuitl Aztec sword

matchlock the first true guns, featuring a metal grip to hold a match for igniting priming powder and a trigger mechanism called a lock

Mexica the ~~Aztec~~ tribe that settled Tenochtitlán

Mixcoatl Cloud Snake, Chichimec father of Quetzalcoatl, patron god of Tlaxaca and Huexotzinco

Mixtec Indian people of northern and western Oaxaca

Motecuhzoma (*c.* 1468–1520) also known as Moctezuma and Montezuma, sixth emperor of Mexico, and second of that name. Reigned 1502–20. Son of Axayacatl. Deposed and died under mysterious circumstances (probably stoned by a mob) while a prisoner of the Spaniards

morion distinctive crested, brimmed helmet

Moors Islamic peoples of Spain

Nahua population of Indian people living throughout central Mexico, the Aztecs were [may have been] a branch of the Nahuas

Nahuatl language of the Nahuas

Nezahualcoyotl famous tlatoani of Texcoco

nextlaualli Aztec term for sacrifice, meaning literally "debt paying"

Reconquista the "reconquest" of the Iberian peninsula by Ferdinand and Isabella

Quetzalcoatl Toltec culture hero of kingdoms throughout central and southern Mexico

Tarascan Indian people of Michoacán, more properly known as Purepecha

tecuhtli land-owning ~~Aztec~~ [Mexihca] lord

telpochcalli Aztec young men's house-warrior school

Tenochtitlán capital city of the Mexica Aztec

Tentlil (also called Teuhtlilli, Teudile or Tendile). Mexican diplomat and administrator over the Totonac vassalage, who first met Cortés on the coast. Vanishes from history after Cortés moves into the interior

tepoztopilli ~~Aztec~~ [Mexihca] halberd

tercio 16th-century Spanish army unit comprising 250 men

Tetlepanquetzal King of Tacuba (Tlacopan) tortured with Cuauhtémoc

tilmatli a broad rectangular weaving worn by the ~~Aztecs~~ [Mexihcas] as a cape or poncho

tlatoani "speaker," high ranking tecuhtli

tonalpouqui ~~Aztec~~ [Mexihca] soothsayer

tzitzimitl ~~Aztec~~ [Mexihca] demon

xicolli a short fringed jacket worn by ~~Aztec~~ [Mexihca] priests

xiquipilli ~~Aztec~~ [Nahuatl] term for a unit of 8,000 men

Zapotec Indian people of Oaxaca

INDEX

Acamapichtli 26
Acapulco 31
adarga (shield) **41**, 46
Aguilar, Alonso de 99, 111, 136, 138–9, 141, 146
Aguilar, Jerónimo de 100
Ahuitzotl 31, 65
Aldrete, Julián 152–3
Alvarado, Pedro de 55, 93, **98**, 127, **128**, 129, 132, 144, 145, 155, 159, 162
Amadís de Gaula (Spanish romantic novel) 53–4
Amecameca 111
Anacoana 7
"Anonymous Conquistador" 56–7
Antilles 38
Anton (Cortés's agent) **157**, **160**
Aragón 7, 17, 34
Arawaks 7, 9
arcabuz (gun) 50
Arias de Ávila, Pedro 25
Arizona 160
armet (helmet) 45–6
armor
  Aztec 69–70, **71**, **72**
  Spanish **41**, **42**, 43–6
Atahualpa 136, 163
atlatl (spear thrower) 65, **66**, 67, **68**
atole (intoxicating drink) 77
Atonal, Lord **23**, 28, 83
Axayacatl 28, 31, 63, 120
axes 67
Ayotzingo 112
Azcapotzalco 26
Aztecs
  acrobats **151**
  agriculture 78
  calendar stone **116**
  education 58–9, 62
  empire, expansion of 26–8, 31
  fatalism of 9, 91
  first contacts with 19, 21

human sacrifice 87, 88, **88**
omens 91, **111**
origins of 21–2
religious festivals 62–3, 91
royal marriages 76
rule of 83
social structure 73
tributes paid to **74**
Triple Alliance 26, 80
Aztecs: warriors **28**, **33**
  ambushes **85**
  armor 69–70, **71**, **72**
  banners and flags **75**
  battlelines **64**
  campaign and supply 77–84
  chain of command 82
  combat 84–6
  communications 84
  dress and distinction 71–7
  invasion columns **79**
  musicians, use of **84**
  myths, use of 87
  organization 80
  prowess 56–7
  and sorcery 83–4
  training 62–5
  weapons 65–9, **66**
Azúa 21

Balboa, Vasco Núñez de 52, 136, 157, 162
baldrics 47
ball games 63
Bancroft, Hubert Howe 33
barbute (helmet) 45
battle wagons **44**
Becerra, Bartolomé 56
Becerra de Durán, Teresa 55–6
Becerrillo (Spanish dog) 20
Black Berthold 48
bows and arrows 65, **66**
breeches 42–3
Brevísimia relación de la destrucción de las Indias (Las Casas) 123
brigandine (protective vest) **41**, 46

broadswords 47, **47**
burgonet (helmet) **39**, **41**, 46

cabasset (helmet) **41**, 45
Cacama (Cacamatzin), King of Texcoco 112, 114,
    121, 125
cacaxtli (carrying frame) **58**
caciques (local kings) 136, 168
Cajamarca 163
calmecac (school) 58, 62, 63, 73
calpulli (town district) 22, 58
Camaxtli *see* Mixcoatl
Campeche 21
Cano, Juan Sebastián del 123
Cape Cruz 95
caps 43
caravels 37–8
carracks 37
casque helmets **43**
Castile 7, 17, 33
celata (helmet) **41**, 45
Cellini, Benvenuto 139
Cempoala **100**, 102, 103, 104, **126**
    battle of (May 1520) 127, 129
Cerignola, battle of (1503) 35–6, 37
chain mail 46
Chalco 28, 112
chapel de fer (helmet) **41**, 45
Chapultepec 26, 60, 120, 145
Charlemagne 38
Charles V (King of Spain) **122**
    and the Americas 122–3
    and arms manufacture 50
Chiapas 31
Chichimecs 22
chimalli (shield) 69
Chimalpopoca 26
chinampas (artificial islands) 22, 60
chocolate (*xocalatl*) 116
Cholula 28, **103**, 105, 108–11
Cihuacoatl (Snake Woman) 82
Clouet, Jean 139
clubs 67
Coanacoch 125

coatepantli (defensive bastion) 26
Coatepec 87
Coatlicue (Lady Serpent Skirt) 87
Coatzacoalcos 55
Cocijoeza 31
Codex Mendoza 170
Coixtlahuaca: siege of (1458) **23**, 28, 80, 83
Colima 154
Colombia 162
Columbus, Christopher **19**
    and Española 7
    first voyage (1492–93) 17–18
    on gold 9
    innovations of 37–8
Columbus, Diego 9
conch shells 84, **86**
Conquistadores
    armor **41**, **42**, 43–6
    banner **96**
    in battle **32**
    capture and sacrifice of 145, **146**
    character 33
    clothing 39–43, **41**
    fighting tactics 50–1
    gunners **93**
    horses **38**
    knights **38**, 45
    landing of **95**, 100–5
    religious motivation 9
    sailors **38**
    and treasure 121, 137, 150, 152–3
    weapons 46–51
copilli (conical cap) **61**
Córdoba, Francisco Hernández de 19, 21, 53
Córdoba, Gonzalo Fernández de 36–7, 50
Coronado, Francisco Vásquez de 157, 160
Cortés, Doña Catalina 158–9
Cortés, Hernán **8**
    on Aztec gods 120–1
    Aztec gods, violation of 125–6
    and Aztec treasure 121, 137, 150, 152–3
    background 21, 34
    at Cempoala 127, 129
    at Cholula 108–11

and Doña Marina 99
later life 159
Motecuhzoma, death of 132, 136
Motecuhzoma, first meeting with 114–15
Motecuhzoma, imprisonment of 121
at Otumba 141
preparations for voyage 93–7
rebuilding of Mexico 155
reputation 157–9
route of **97**
on slavery 154
Tenochtitlán, advance to (1519) **106**, **107**, 110–14
Tenochtitlán, retreat from (1520) **13**, **92**, 136, 137–9, **138**
Tenochtitlán, siege of (1521) 144–50
Tlaxcala, march to **53**, 140–1
and Tlaxcalteca **104**, 105–8
and Totonacs 102–5
and Velásquez 21, 93, 94–5, 102
veneration as a god **98–9**
Cortés, Martín 99
Cortés de Monroy, Don Martín 21
Coyoacán 113, 144, 150, 155
Coyolxauhqui 87
Coyolxauhqui Stone **30**
Cozumel 100
creoles 163
Crónica de la Nueva España (López de Gómara) 56
crossbows 47–8, **49**
cuahchic 57
cuahchique ("berserkers") 73
Cualpopoca 121, 126
cuauhololli (club) 67
cuauhpilli (commander) 82
Cuauhtémoc **149**
  becomes emperor 144
  capture of 149–50
  death of 159
  on Honduras expedition 159
  as national hero 164–5
  and siege of Tenochtitlán 144, 146
  torture of 152–3
  troops 154

Cuba: invasion of 9, 19, **20**
cuextecatl (trophy uniform) 72, 73
cuextecatl soldiers 60, **61**, 64
Cuitláhuac 114, 125, 132, 144
Cuitláhuac Causeway 112–13
culebrina (cannon) 51
Culhuacán: Aztec conquest of **16**
Cuzco 163

Darien (Panama) 19, 52
Díaz del Castillo, Bernal 44–5
  on advance to Mexico 113–14, 115
  background 51–2
  on capture of Cuauhtémoc 150
  on Cortés 56
  on Doña Marina 99, 101
  expeditions 52–5
  memoirs 51, 56, 93
  Motecuhzoma, on death of 136
  Motecuhzoma, opinion of 54–5
  on Tlatelolco 120
  wealth 163
Díaz del Castillo, Francisco 51–2
Diego, Juan 166, 170
dogs: use by Conquistadores **20**, 95–6
doublets 40–2
Durán, Diego 64, 76, 132
Durán, Juan 56

Eastern Nahuas 26, 28, 83, 91
Ecuador 162
ehuatl (tunic) 70, **71**, **90**
El Cid 38
encomienda 7–8, 154–5, **160**, 168
escopeta (gun) 50
Española (Haiti-Santo Domingo) 7–8, 9
espingarda (gun) 50
Esquivel, Juan de 9
Extremadura 34, **36**

falconets **49**, **50**, 51
Ferdinand, King: and *Reconquista* 7, 17, 34, 36
Florentine Codex (Sahagún) 169–70
Florida 19, 163

"flower wars" 63
Francis I of France 139

Garay, Francisco de 126, 154, 159
Garigliano, battle of (1504) 37
gold: search for 9
gowns 42
Granada 7, 17
Great Mixtón War 162
Grijalva, Juan de 19, 21, 53, 93, 95
Guanajuato 166
Guatemala 55, 56, 159
Guatémoc see Cuauhtémoc
Guerrero 26, 31
Guerrero, Gonzalo 100, 160
guns 48, 50–1
Guzmán, Domingo de **168**
Guzmán, Nuño de 160

halberds
    Aztec **58**, **66**, 68
    Spanish **49**
helmets
    Aztec 69, **71**, **78**
    Spanish **41**, **43**, 45–6
Historia general de las cosas de la Nueva España
    (Sahagún) 169–70
History of Mexico (Bancroft) 33
The History of the Conquest of Mexico (Prescott)
    21, 166
The History of the Indies of New Spain (Durán)
    76
Holguín, García 149
Holy Roman Empire 122
Honduras 19, 55, 159
hose 42
Huaxtecs 28, 63, 72, 85
Huaxyacac (Oaxaca City) 83
Huexotzinco 28, 31, 105, 111
huey tlatoque ("great speakers") 26, 73, 80, 82,
    113
Huitzilihuitl 26
Huitzilopochtli (war god) **7**, 26, 28, 30, 87, 91,
    104, 117, 120

huitzinahuatl (commanding officer) 73
Humboldt, Alexander von 21

ichcahuipilli (armor jackets) 46, 70, **71**, 73
Indians: treatment of 123
infantry squares **37**
Isabella, Queen: and *Reconquista* 7, 17, 36
Isla Mujeres 100
Itzapalapa 113, 145, 146
Itzapalapa Causeway 114
Itzcoatl 26
Ixtacíhuatl 110

Jalisco 31, 159
Jamaica 9, 19
Jaramillo, Juan 99
jerkins 42
John Paul II, Pope 170
Juárez, Benito 165–6
Juárez, Catalina 21
Juárez, Juan 21

Künsthistorische Museum, Vienna 150

La Malinche see Marina, Doña
La Noche Triste (1520) 51, 55, **133**, **134–5**, 138–9
La Plata 157
Lake Chalco 112–13
Lake Patzcuaro 31
Lake Texcoco 22, **27**, 60
Lake Xochimilco 113
lances 47
Las Casas, Bartolomé de 123
Las Casas, Francisco de **168**
Leonardo da Vinci 139
lombarda (cannon) 51
López de Gómara, Francisco 56, 99, 121, 129

macuahuitl (sword) **66**, 67–9, **73**
macehualtin (commoners) 73
Magellan, Ferdinand 123
Marina, Doña 53–4, **98**, 99, 101, **104**, 108, 121
matchlock muskets **47**, **49**, 50
matlaxopilli (net-bird claw) **137**

Maximilian, Archduke 165–6

Maxixcatzin, Lord **137**

Maxtla 26

maxtlatl (loin cloth) **60**

Maya 19, 159–60

Mendoza, Antonio de 55, **169**, 170

Merced, Father de la 54

Merida 112

mestizo 99, 163–4

Metropolitan Cathedral, Mexico City 114

Mexica (tribe) 22, 26, 60

Mexico

  architecture 166

  and Aztec civilization 166

  caste system 164–5

  Catholicism 166–7

  maps **10**

  nationalism 163

  relations with Spain 164–5

  Valley of (1519) **27**

Mexico City **156**, **162**

  see also Tenochtitlán

Michoacán 31, 153–4, 160

Mixcoatl (god) 105

Mixtecs 26, 28, 83, 91

Moctezuma *see* Motecuhzoma

Moctezuma, Eduardo Matos 30

momoyactli (fan) 73

Monte de Piedad, Mexico City 114

Montejo, Francisco de 102, 122–3, 159–60

Montezuma *see* Motecuhzoma

Moors 17, 34

Morelos 26

morion (helmet) 45

Motecuhzoma I 26, 28

Motecuhzoma II **77**

  death 132, 136

  and expansion of Aztec empire 31

  expectation of arrival of Conquistadores 91

  failure to crush Spaniards 112

  gifts to Cortés 102, 110, 111

Nahuas *see* Eastern Nahuas

Naples 34

Napoleon III 165

Narváez, Pánfilo de 9, 123, 126–7, 129, 160, 163

National Palace, Mexico City 114

Navarre 17

New Granada 157

New Laws 123, 155

New Mexico 160

New Spain 157

New World 18

nextlaualli (sacred debt) 87

Nezahualcoyotl 26, 28, **79**

Nicaragua 19

Oaxaca 28, 31, 55, 105, 155

obsidian blades 68–9

Ocotelolco 105

"Old Melchor" 100

oleander 83–4

Olíd, Cristóbal de 93, 144, 154, 159

Oñate, Cristóbal de 159

Ordaz, Diego 111

Orteguilla (Cortés's page) 126

Otumba, battle of (July 1520) 140–1

Ovando, Friar Nicolás de 7–8, 21

pamitl (flag) 73

Pánuco 121, 126, 154

pasabolante (cannon) 51

Paul III, Pope 123

peninsulares (native Spanish) 163

Peru 157, 162–3

Pilón 95

pipiltin (lords) 73

Pizarro, Francisco 34, 136, 157, 162–3

Pizarro de Altamirano, Doña Catalina 21

Plumed Serpent Temple, Teotihuacán **24–5**

Ponce de Léon, Juan 9, 20, 136, 163

Pontonchán 100

Popocatépetl 110–11

Portugal 17

Prescott, William H. 21, 166

priests: costumes **81**

Puebla 28, 105

Pueblo 160
Puente de Alvarado, Mexico City 145
Puerto Rico 9, 19
Puertocarrero, Alonso Hernández 102, 122–3
Purépacha, king of 160

Quecholli festival 65
Quetzalcoatl (Plumed Serpent god) **24–5**, **59**, 62, 91, 99, 104
Quiahuiztlan 105

rapiers 47
rattlesnakes 116
rerebraces (armor) **41**
Rio Grijalva 100
Roland 38

Sahagún, Bernardino de 109, 112, 132, 167, **167**, 169–70
salades (helmets) **41**, 45
San Juan de Ulúa 101, 164
Sandoval, Gonzalo 55, 93, 126–7, 129, 144–5
Santa Cruz de Tlatelcolo, college-convent of 162
Santa Maria, Domingo de **168**
Segura de la Frontera 141, 144
Seminara, battle of (1495) 35, 37
shields
   Aztec **17**, **66**, **67**, 69, **70**
   Spanish **41**, 46
slings 65
smallpox **127**, 129, 144
Snake Mountain 87
Soconusco 31
Sonora 160
Soto, Hernando de 157, 163
Spain
   nobility 34
   persecution of non-Catholics 17, **18**
   Reconquista 7, 17, 34, 36
Spanish army
   in Italy 35–6, 37
   knights 34
   men-at-arms **35**
Spanish Main 9

spears 65, **66**, 67
stirrups **52**
Sublimis Deus (papal bull) 123
surgery **54**
Swiss mercenaries 35, 39
swords
   Aztec **66**, 67–9
   Spanish 46–7, **47**, **49**

Tabasco 100
Tacuba 28, 153
Tapia, Andrés 106, 117, 125
Tarascans 26, 31, 153–4
tassets (thigh armor) **41**
tecociauacatl **29**
Tehuantepec 28, 31, 55
telpochcalli (school) **57**, 58, 62, 63, 72
telpochtlato (military instructor) 58, 62
temilotl (hairstyle) 69
Temple of the Sun, Teotihuacán **130–1**
Temple of the Warriors, Tollan **101**
Templo Mayor (Great Temple) **14**, 26, 28, 30, **115**, 117, **118–19**, **142**, **148**, **165**
Tenayuca: Aztec conquest of **16**
Tenochtitlán (Mexico City)
   character of 22, 26
   chimpanas 22, 60
   Cortés's retreat from (1520) **13**, **92**, 136, 137–9, **138**
   founding of **16**, 22
   Great Temple **14**, 26, 28, 30, **115**, 117, **118–19**, **142**, **148**, **165**
   maps **110**, **117**
   menagerie 116–17
   siege of (1520) 132, 136
   siege of (1521) **6**, **143**, 144–50, **147**, **152**
   smallpox epidemic (1521) **127**, 144
   temple and plaza precincts 60, 62
   Toxcatl massacre 129, 132
Tentlil 102
teosinte (plant) 77
Teotihuacán **130–1**
Tepanapa 109
Tepanecs 26

Tepeaca 141
Tepeticpac 105
Tepeyac 166–7
Teposcolula 28
tepoztopilli (halberd) **58**, **66**, 68
tetecuhtin (petty-kings) 73, **82**, 105
Tetlepanquetzal, King of Tacuba 153
Teuhtlilli *see* Tentlil
Texcoco 26, 154
Tezcatlipoca (god) 62, 91, 104, 112, 120
Tezozomoc 26
Thomas, Hugh 157, 158
ticocyahuacatl (commanding officer) 73
Tilantongo 28
tilmatli (cape) 43, **60**, 73–4, 76
Tizatlan 105
Tizoc 31
Tlacaelel 26, 28, 76, 82
tlacatecatl (commanding officer) **29**, 73
Tlachihualtepl ("Hill of the Idol"), Cholula **103**, 108
tlacochcalcatl (commanding officer) **29**, 73
Tlacopán 26
Tlacopán (Tacuba) Causeway 114, **134–5**, 138, 145
tlahuiztli (body suit) **61**, 72–3
Tlaloc (storm god) **7**, **24–5**, 26, 28, 62, 117, **124**
tlamemehque (porters) 80
Tlatelolco, Mexico City 117, 120, **162**
Tlaxcala 28, 31, 140, 141
  Cortés's march to **53**
  Manuscript 44
Tlaxcalteca **32**, 63, 65, 91, 144, 146–7, 150
  baptism of lords **153**
  and Cortés **104**, 105–8
  war banners, burning of **158**
Tlaxiaco 28
Tlazolteotl (goddess) 73
Tollan 87, **101**
Toltecs 22, 87
tonalpouqui (soothsayer) 57–8
Tonantzin (goddess) 167
Tonatiuh (sun god) 88, 99
Tordesillas, treaty of (1494) 139
Totonacs 19, 21, 28, 91, 101, 102–5, 122–3

Totoquihuaztli 28
Toxcatl massacre 129, 132
Triple Alliance 26, 80
True History of the Conquest of New Spain (Díaz del Castillo) 51, 56
Tubanama 136
Tula 22, 104, 105
Tututepec 80
Tzintzuntzan 31
tzompantli (skull rack) **14**, **16**, 117, **119**

uitznauatl **29**
Umbría, Gonzalo de 117

Vaca, Cabeza de 160
vambraces (armor) **41**
Velásquez, Diego de Silva y 9, **94**
  commissioning of expeditions 19, 21, 93, 94-5, 123
  and Cortés 21, 94–5
  seizing of hostages 136
Velásquez de Cuéllar, Diego 20
Veracruz 21, 28, **55**, 101, 164
Villa Rica 51, 102, 121, 126, 141, 142
Virgin of Guadalupe 166, 170

weapons
  Aztec 65–9, **66**
  Spanish 46–51

xicolli (cotton jacket) 43, 73
Xipe Totec (war god) 62, 120
xiquipilli (regiment) 71, 80
Xochimilco 63, 144, 146
xopilli (claw) 73

Yucatán Caste War (1847) 112
Yucatán Peninsula 21, 100, 154, 159–60
Yuste, Juan 144

Zapotecs 26, 28, 31, 83, 91
Zautla 105
Zócalo plaza 114
Zumárraga, Bishop Juan de 162, 170